**FLATIRON
BOOKS**

NEW YORK

PANTSUIT NATION

Edited by Libby Chamberlain

www.flatironbooks.com

Designed by Jonathan Bennett

The Library of Congress Cataloging-in-Publication Data is available upon request.

ISBN 978-1-250-15332-6 (hardcover)

ISBN 978-1-250-15333-3 (e-book)

Our books may be purchased in bulk for promotional, educational, or business use. Please contact your local bookseller or the Macmillan Corporate and Premium Sales Department at 1-800-221-7945, extension 5442, or by e-mail at MacmillanSpecialMarkets@macmillan.com.

First Edition: May 2017

10 9 8 7 6 5 4 3 2 1

To Pantsuit Nation
Glimmers in the dark

CONTRIBUTORS
WRITING

CONTRIBUTORS

PHOTOGRAPHY

JAMIE THROWER VI, 108, 202 DAVID SCHULMAN VIII, 258, 266 *MICHELE GUARNIERI* X, 248 (TOP RIGHT) J. LINDSEY LINGENFELTER XIII *JINA SUNG* XIV REGAN MORO 1 *C.C.P.* 3 ADINA DAVIDSON 4 *SHIRLEY MCCLURE* 7 WARDAH KHAN 9 *RUTH MARIMO* 10 MOLLY WERNICK 11 *THE STILES FAMILY* 12 PAUL TOEPFER PHOTOGRAPHY 15 *SMEETA MAHANTI* 16 CHRISTINA LIEW 18 *CLARICE MCINTOSH* 22 TOBY GRUBMAN & LOIS VILLEMAIRE 23 *GRETCHEN KIRBY* 24 ANDREA MINTON 26 *BERNADETTE EVANS* 27 REBECCA 28 *SAL D.* 30 BROOKE BOLING 31 *CINDA DANH* 34 KRISTEN MARTIN 36 *PAM GORDON* 38 APRIL K. HOOVER 39 *ALBERT* 40 AMY PATEL 42 *MASHEED K. ROCKWELL* 43 MELODY TARRO 45 *J BRIZENDINE PHOTOGRAPHY* 46 REV. LILLIAN J. BUCKLEY 48 *BOUA XIONG-ROY* 50 JENNY 53 *LOLA HAKE* 56 CLAUDIA RAMIREZ-HOLZBAUER 57 *AMANDA DELP CONNELL/A.M. PHOTOGRAPHY* 58 SHERRILYN MCCOY PECORELLA 60 *ROSEANNE GATTO* 61 DEANNA TEASLEY 63 JAKE GRAVBOT 66 LEIAH ROBBINS 68 *BRENDAN MCLAUGHLIN* 70 CRISTINA LOPEZ 73 *CHIP SOMODEVILLA/ GETTY IMAGES NEWS* 76 BARBARA KINNEY/HILLARY FOR AMERICA 80 *EMILY ELCONIN* 82 MINA NEUMÜLLER MALHOTRA 84 *SUSAN WILLIAMS* 87 SEAN BROWN 88 *NAAMAL DE SILVA* 90 TONY MACK 91 *LINDSAY WOODS* 93 SARAH GORMLEY 94 *NICK GOMEZ* 96 BONNIE LAPEÉ 98 *SAKENA SHAMBERGER* 99 BETHANY JOHNSON 100 *EMILY BOVE* 103 MKS 104 *SARAH* 105 HERB CONDE-PARLATO 106 *ELISE HANNA* 110 FATIMA FALL 112 *LIBBY SAUTER* 113 KAREN SEIFERT 114 *BRENT W. HOPKINS* 117 ELISABET 118 LAUREN KROHN 120 *KRITTER* 123 JILL MEYER 124 *ROBIN SEWELL DAUM* 126 GINA GLORIOSO 127 RANDI FREUNDLICH 129 *RAINBOW BELLS* 130 JONATHAN BRANDEIS 134 *ALEX H.* 138 MONET HOLMES 141 *PENNY GODWIN* 142 BETHANY JANA 144, 248 (TOP LEFT) *COSTAS STERGIOU,* 150 DEENA 152 *TIFFANY YIZAR* 153 SAFANA SHEIKH AHMED 154 *AIXA PEREZ-PRADO* 155 KIT FULLER 156 *MAJ, ALEX* 159 ANNA ASTVATSATURIAN TURCOTTE 160 *NAOMI WHEELESS* 161 CYNTHYA PORTER 162 *ADAM HAMILTON-FERGUSON* 164 SHARON BLAKE 165 *ANGELA L. OWENS/GIGI MANN IMAGES* 166 JENNY MYERS 168 *MERISSA LYNN PHOTOGRAPHY* 170 ENIS HUSKIC 178 *JESSICA MCCLELLAN* 181 LEANNA J. GABLE 183 *KIM RODRIGUEZ* 184 BARBARA LA VALLEUR 186 *ADACHI PIMENTEL* 190 LINDSAY POVEROMO-JOLY 192 *GINA GIANETTO* 197 SHANNON GRANT 199 *WHITNEY AYMAR/WHITNEY ROSE PHOTOGRAPHY* 200 HUNTER H. RUDD 206 *LAILA JABER* 208 JAN TOMAS 210 *HEATHER WILLIAMS* 212 J.A. 213 *KAHAIA CHANTAL PHOTOGRAPHY* 214 ZELL GOLEMAN 217 *JESSICA D'ONOFRIO* 218 AARON R. RIEDER 220 *JULIE CLARKE/MEMORIES REMAIN PHOTOGRAPHY* 224 JAMES W. GRADY, JR./ELITE EXPRESSIONS PHOTOGRAPHY 227 *NJERI MILLNER* 228 RICK PASETTO 230 *KHRISTY K. PRESTON* 233 NUREN HAIDER 234 *MARK BREAULT NEUBAUER* 236 PATRICIA A. ROOS 239 *KEITH SCOTT* 240 CHARLES BRICE/BRICE MEDIA 243 *LAUREN ASHLEY HOWARD, ESQ.* 244 KENNEDY CARROLL/THERIPPLE.ORG 246 *NEHA WADEKAR* 248 (BOTTOM), 265 MONICA WILLIAMS 249 (TOP) *KELSEY MCGREGOR* 249 (BOTTOM) CHRISTINA GANDOLFO 253 *RAJIB C.* 254 JAMES EVERETT PHOTOGRAPHY 257 *MATTHEW EARLE* 262 KATHLEEN SHARP 268 *EMILIE INC. PHOTOGRAPHY* 270 **ELECTION DAY COLLAGE 74-75 (LEFT TO RIGHT, TOP TO BOTTOM):** ANNE HARRIGAN *RYAN TYMENSKY & DOMINIC VALENTINO LE FORT* MICHELLE CARTAYA DENNIS KWAN RANDI FREUNDLICH *AMY PATEL* LINDSAY HITE *TORONDA SINDLER (TOP)* ANONYMOUS (BOTTOM) *ANNIE* REBECCA ICKES (TOP) *JULIE LIPPERT (MIDDLE)* ERIN C. SUTHERLAND (BOTTOM) *CAITLIN FREY* LUISA ERICKSON *JASMINE R. (TOP)* KRISTIN (BOTTOM) *EDISON LEE (TOP)* ERIN LITTLE (BOTTOM) *EMILIE INC. (TOP)* AMEENAH NADIRAH (BOTTOM) *JULIE LIPPERT* **MARCH COLLAGE 250-251 (LEFT TO RIGHT, TOP TO BOTTOM):** EMILY SHAPIRO MELISSA MARR *ADITEE MANÉ* LINDA KAY COTTRELL *VALERIE PLESCH* MELINA B. HARTLEY *CHANTILLE DE LOS REYES* ABBEY & PATRICIA HALL *JENNIFER S. EASTERDAY* JULIE FISER SILJE YASMINE YADIRA DEBBIE KEATLEY *ADINA DAVIDSON* LARISSA KLAZINGA *ANNE PRUETT* LIZ OGLESBY *ZORA* MEAGAN M. TURNER *LAURIE ALDERSON* REGINAH MAKO & RIGHTS AND DEMOCRACY *BROOKE MOBLEY* LAILA KAISER *KIM REHBERG* CADDIE JACKSON

INTRODUCTION

The book you are holding in your hands is a time capsule. It's also an experiment in the power of collective storytelling. And it's a rallying cry. It grew out of something as improbable and ephemeral as a secret Facebook group for thirty friends who were planning to wear pantsuits to the polls on November 8, 2016. What it becomes next is up to you.

Pantsuit Nation began on October 20, the day after the third presidential debate. Craving an online space that was free of vitriol, fake news, and the abusive commentary that had become commonplace over the course of the 2016 election, I uploaded a photo of Hillary Clinton, radiant in her white pantsuit from the night before, and wrote the following description for the group: "Wear a pantsuit on November 8—you know why."

The idea to wear a pantsuit to the polls was inspired by a conversation with my friend, Caddie. While watching the debate, Caddie overheard a young woman say something along the lines of "Ugh. Another ugly pantsuit." It was less than two weeks after a video had surfaced of the Republican nominee bragging about sexual assault, and yet the conversation turned, as it had so often in the months leading up to that debate, to Secretary Clinton's clothing. The volume of her voice. Whether she was smiling not enough or too much. The height of her heels and the cut of her jacket.

I didn't own a pantsuit at the time. It didn't matter. I knew that more than any other campaign pin, slogan, or logo, the pantsuit symbolized this moment in history, and I wanted to wear that symbol—to embrace it and embody it and celebrate it—when I went to cast my vote in that historic election. It turns out I wasn't the only one.

Within one day of creating the group and inviting a handful of my own friends to join, it exploded to more than 24,000 members. Friends invited friends by the thousands to a "secret" group where they could unabashedly support Secretary Clinton. Where they didn't have to hide their excitement or temper their enthusiasm. "I've found my people!" and "I knew you were all out there somewhere!" were familiar refrains in the group in those first few days. There were few rules, but there was one I was adamant about: in the words of Michelle Obama, we would "Go high." Posts that disparaged either candidate or their supporters would not be tolerated. There was plenty of that in other spaces and I wanted to create something different.

While there were a number of memes and pro-Clinton articles being shared in the beginning, something else started happening as well. Members, particularly women, began sharing stories about what this election meant to them. Stories about workplace harassment, about mothers and grandmothers with great aspirations and far-reaching ambitions who were limited not by their creativity or talent but by their gender. Lawyers and teachers and scientists posted in the group about the fight to wear pants, literally, and about the fight for what the pantsuit represented to them: equality, empowerment, and autonomy.

We read about "Hank," a TWA stewardess (as they were then called) who attended Stanford Medical School in 1938 and gave up a career in medicine to get married, only to find herself stationed at Pearl Harbor with a six-month-old baby on December 7, 1941. Her granddaughter, Susan (page 32), dedicated her vote for Secretary Clinton to four generations of women in her family, starting with Hank and ending with her own daughter.

Sian (page 70) also posted about her grandmother, who raised four children in a tiny apartment in Shanghai before immigrating to the United States. In 2001, standing at her kitchen window in New York City's Chinatown, she "watched the World Trade Center fall" and then "draped their apartment in American flags and memorabilia, much like the rest of the city's residents."

These stories, which were posted in the group by the hundreds and then by the thousands, were deeply personal and yet profoundly universal. They seemed, at times, to have a generative power of their own— the more people shared, the more others were inspired to do the same, so that stories begat stories. This was the first glimpse I had of *collective* storytelling, where the impact of hundreds of thousands and then millions of people gathering together in a virtual space to speak and listen was something unique and worth preserving.

Leading up to the election, the size of the group swelled to 100,000, then to 250,000, and then surpassed 1,000,000 members on November 5. The stories grew, too, not just in number but in scope. We heard from first-generation Americans, from people of color, from immigrants and refugees,

from people with disabilities, and from members of the LGBTQIA community about how, for them, the outcome of this election could mean the difference between acceptance and rejection based on their identity, their families, their ancestry, whom they loved, and how they worshipped. The pantsuit, it turns out, could represent everything from a doctor's scrubs to a military uniform to a hijab.

We read Ileana's story (page 44) of being the daughter of Cuban immigrants and living in the "heart of the South," where she cast her vote "for the tens of thousands who have lost their lives to suicide or hate crimes based on their mental health issues or bullying stemming from their gender identity or sexual orientation." Jenny (page 52) wrote about being a sexual assault survivor and voting "for my daughters and yours." There was a rising chorus of voices, beautiful and complex in their differences, but also inspiring in their shared commitment to love, kindness, and inclusion.

Hundreds of thousands and then millions of people gathering together in a virtual space to speak and listen was something unique and worth preserving.

Pantsuit Nation was also a catalyst for action. With help from a growing team of volunteers (many of whom simply sent me a brief message asking, "Can I help?" to which I almost always responded, "Yes, please!"), we organized a fund-raising drive for the Clinton campaign, which raised more than $200,000 in a matter of days. We set up a call team for phone banking, which was ranked in the top ten nationally on the weekend before the election. Members posted about canvassing and texting undecided voters and volunteering to drive elderly neighbors to their polling locations, often crediting the stories within the group for providing them the motivation they needed to put in those long hours.

The storytellers in our midst, whose voices thrum against the tides of injustice, are our most powerful agents of change.

On Election Day, we added one million members, going from two to three million in the span of about twenty-four hours. My vision for an army of pantsuited warriors taking to the polls unfolded before our eyes, as tens of thousands of people sent in selfies from polling stations around the country (pages 74-75). I put on my own (hastily purchased) pantsuit and went with my husband, daughter, and son to vote after gathering with about fifty pantsuited residents of our small Maine town for a photo.

Then we watched together in the early morning of November 9 as our collective hopes were dashed.

In her concession speech, Secretary Clinton issued the ultimate call to action to our members: "And to the millions of volunteers, community leaders, activists, and union organizers who knocked on doors, talked to their neighbors, posted on Facebook— *even in secret, private Facebook sites*—I want everybody coming out from behind that and make sure your voices are heard going forward."

Voices. Stories. Neighbors.

Organizers. Activists. Leaders. The relationship between storytelling and activism is nothing new. Stories are fuel. They are the why. Stories give meaning to action and meaningful action is the only way to drive long-term, sustainable change. From Anne Frank to Mamie Till to Delores Huerta to Christy Brown to Marsha P. Johnson to Alicia Garza, the storytellers in our midst, whose voices thrum against the tides of injustice, are our most powerful agents of change. What Pantsuit Nation showed us in those first weeks and months after the election is that we are *all* storytellers. And so, we are all powerful. Beyond our own imagining.

For anyone who still doubts the impact a story can have on the world, who thinks that stories are mere feel-good pats on the back, I invite you, with all my heart, to read what follows in these pages. For many of the people whose stories are gathered in this book, particularly for those who come from historically marginalized communities,

The stories collected here are a clarion call for intersectional feminists of every class, shade, gender, nationality, religion, and ethnicity to join together in resistance.

telling a story is an act of incredible courage in and of itself. Shortly after November 8, Adrian (page 174), a former Marine Sergeant and father to three young children, wrote to Pantsuit Nation, "I never thought I would feel this way again. Growing up 'different' in a very conservative town was enough for me to want to leave. And now that feeling has resurfaced." Melissa (page 165) posted, "I've spent my life sometimes feeling overlooked, excluded, and underestimated—doing everything I can think of to change the way society views the disabled community. My mantra has always been, 'I'm a person,' and that's never been more true than right now." Pantsuit Nation members, in post after post after post, stood up together in solidarity to declare that our voices would no longer be silenced, that our stories matter, and that a new narrative, one that features the perspectives of those who, like Adrian and Melissa, have long been dismissed or ignored, is coming to light.

For others, stories are shields, building blocks, olive branches. They are Deena's homemade baklava (page 152) and Hanadi's haircut (page 186) and the painted front gate of Bethany's white picket fence (page 100). They are proof that we're not alone, that goodness bubbles up, that, as Maya Angelou declared, "Like dust, we rise." These stories capture small actions that, through amplification, have the power to become a revolution. They might put a smile on your face, but they are just as likely to give you momentary pause, to force you to reconsider an assumption, or to motivate you to extend the grace and generosity you've just read about to someone beyond the confines of a "secret, private Facebook site." Is this effect quantifiable? Probably not, at least not yet. But in the thousands of conversations I've had in the last three months, and in the exchanges I read in Pantsuit Nation every day between members, and in my own life, as I have witnessed injustice or hardship and decided how to respond, there is evidence everywhere that the power of collective storytelling can drive the kind of widespread, organic shift toward compassion and empathy that history tells us is the leading edge of social and political change.

Some stories are mementos, tucked into pockets like Hunter's Purple Heart (page 206) or displayed on the wall like the portrait of Jeff and Nikki (page 166). Stories that reflect back but also demand future action. That implore us to remember, to honor, and to engage. If we can be driven to care about the stories of others, we can be driven to care about the policies that affect them.

Some of the stories in this book have few or no words, but they speak volumes. Some will make you uncomfortable, which is very much by design. Some are like Jia's "pocketful of glitter" (page 200), sparkling moments of light and levity at an otherwise fraught time in our history. They are raw and real and urgent. Individually, they are beautiful. Collectively, they are a mandate.

Pantsuit Nation has become a community of diverse voices allied in resistance, grief, and hope. In the months after the election it has taken on a life beyond Facebook as we launched our website, founded our nonprofits to further the mission of our group, and, of course, collaborated on this book. The conversations I have had with the hundreds of Pantsuit Nation members who submitted their posts for inclusion in the book have only reinforced the idea that storytelling is an essential element of activism. They are committed to taking Secretary Clinton up on her charge to make sure *our* voices are heard going forward.

The stories collected here are arranged roughly in chronological order, as they were posted within the group. Like each of us as individuals, they defy easy categorization and instead open us up to the fullness of what it means to be human. They illustrate, achingly, the effects of systemic racism, ableism, homophobia, and xenophobia, and they are a clarion call for intersectional feminists of every class, shade, gender, nationality, religion, and ethnicity to join together in resistance. They show that Black Lives Matter. They show that love is love is love. They show that our diversity is our strength. They show what was at stake on November 8, 2016, what seemed to have been lost on November 9, and what has, instead, been reasserted as the essential truth and commonality of our values.

As I write this, three months have passed since I started the group. Last weekend, millions of people marched all over the world to protest the inauguration of Donald Trump (page 246). Marchers from Oslo and Buenos Aires and Seoul and St. Louis posted photos and stories in the group, much as voters posted pantsuit selfies by the thousands two months earlier. The context could not have been more different, but the energy was familiar. Collected voices. Strength in numbers. Intersecting identities. The pantsuit, for me, was always a symbol of courage. A uniform that, as unlikely as it seemed at first, brought together a disparate but indelibly united group of people on the side of justice and inclusion.

This is Pantsuit Nation.

LIBBY CHAMBERLAIN
JANUARY, 2017

It took me about four seconds

to realize I was gay, but it took me four years to fully come out of the closet. The thing that finally made me push that door wide open was the Pulse nightclub shooting this past June—I was struck by the bravery of those who died that night, and ashamed at my own fear. I came out fully, received messages of love (mostly), and worked up enough courage to attend my first Pride parade.

I'm with her because of this picture of me at the parade. I'm an optimistic person and I smile often, but do you see that smile? That smile is different. It's one of hard-won self-acceptance and paralyzing truthfulness and, eventually, openness. I've had to fight hard for that smile, and some days I still have to go looking for it.

"The closet" might seem like a metaphor that's solely applicable to the LGBTQIA community, but I don't believe that to be true. We all have thoughts and longings and feelings and desires that don't seem normal, perhaps even those that seem shameful, and so we all live in a type of "closet" from time to time.

I have a nephew who is three years old, whom I love more than anything in the world. I want him and my future kids and your kids and your brother's ex-girlfriend's cousins' kids to grow up in a world where they know that feelings don't fit properly in closets, that closets are dusty and tiny and dark, that closets are no place for a person to live. I want them to share their truths freely and easily, not as an aftershock to some mass tragedy. I don't want their brightest smiles to be so fought for. And that's why I'm with her.

My parents

came here as immigrants seeking a better life for their children and grandchildren.

In the thirty years they have been American citizens, they have never voted. I don't know if it was out of fear or if they simply just did not understand the process.

I am so proud of the people who raised me and the little people I am now raising.

But they have paid their taxes. They have worked themselves to the bone so that my brother and I could go to college and leave college debt-free. They have swallowed any pride and turned their cheek after every insult hurled at them. After every joke that mocked their accented English.

After my husband and I voted with our young boys, they showed their grandparents how to vote for the first time. I am so proud of the people who raised me and the little people I am now raising.

C.C.P., TEXAS

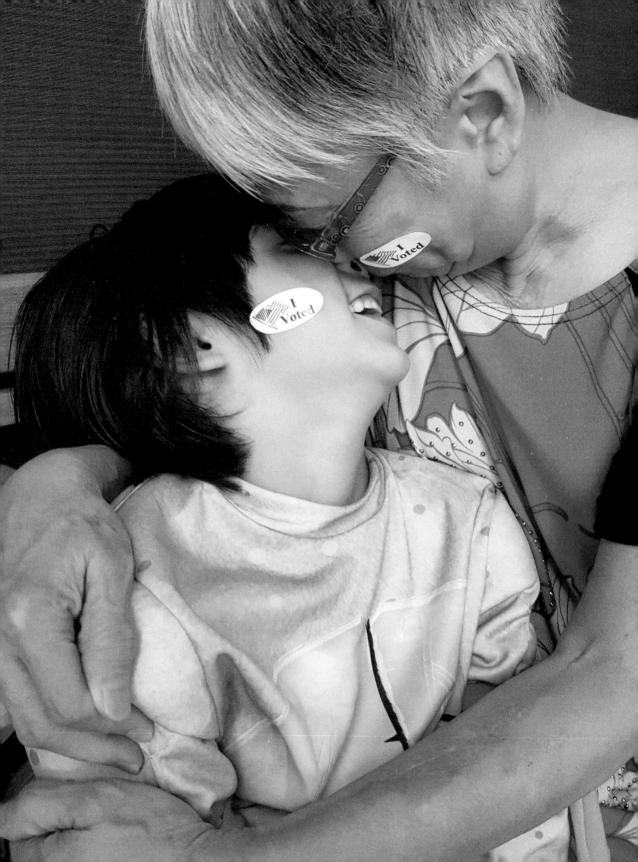

I'm with her for so many reasons

—but my two sweet boys and the two foster children in our home that we hope to one day adopt are at the heart of it for me. I want the four of them to grow up with a president that promotes inclusiveness, respect, strength, hope, and kindness.

The best pantsuit I ever wore

was green, adorned with accomplishments, and finished off with classic jump boots.

I was part of the first gender-integrated Basic Training cycle, which was interesting to say the least. I am also one of the few women that managed to graduate Jump School and stay active in the 82nd Airborne Division, where I was part of the 313th Military Intelligence Battalion.

Every time I heard,
"No...you're just a girl."
I said, "Watch me."

MICAL, NEW YORK

We're with her!

SHIRLEY McCLURE, FLORIDA

I am a Muslim physician, wearing hijab,

born and raised in the US. I am a mother of two lovely boys. I contribute to the good of society on a daily basis.

I cannot imagine a post-Trump world, where my family and I may feel subject to his anti-Muslim sentiment, his racist ideas, a country unsafe for my boys.

As an immigrant

who cannot yet vote in America, and whose children are too young to vote, I want to personally thank each and every one of you who are voting for Hillary for doing so. It means the world to me and my children.

RUTH, NEBRASKA

Last week, before she submitted her absentee ballot, I asked my grandma, "What do you have to say about voting for the first female president?" **"HOORAY!"** she exclaimed. Way to go, Grandma Pearl!

MOLLY, PENNSYLVANIA

I will be voting in a pantsuit on November 8 in memory of my grandma,

Elizabeth Cavanaugh, who proudly told me she was the first woman to wear "slacks" to work on her block. She wanted to be a lawyer, but was sent to secretarial school instead. She took a legal secretary job at a firm where she ended up training all of the newly minted male lawyers. She visited the Supreme Court a few times because her firm represented the Catholic Church in amicus briefs in abortion cases during the time SCOTUS was considering *Roe v. Wade*. She was pro-choice, but was glad to have witnessed that important moment in history.

She drove herself from Pennsylvania to New York City to attend my law school graduation in 2006, despite being very ill at the time. It was only the second time in my life I saw her cry. The first was when my grandpa died. She assured me it was tears of joy, watching her granddaughter have the opportunity she never had.

I will also have my grandpa Jimmy on my mind in that voting booth. For a few years, he was the only registered Democrat in his whole town in rural Pennsylvania, close to Scranton, where HRC's grandfather worked in a lace mill. The local Republican club used to invite my grandpa to their picnics just to have someone to argue with, and he went! I remember him saying, "I'm not afraid of those idiots and they make good barbecue."

Despite barely finishing 8th grade, because he left school to drive a cab to earn money for his family, he was one of the smartest people I ever knew. I remember him sitting me down on his knee explaining the Iran-Contra scandal when I was eight as we watched the news together. It was the first time I took an interest in politics, and I've been kind of obsessed ever since. He also told me that good Irishmen always vote Democrat. I asked why and he gave me a lesson on the Kennedys and the good things Democrats did for hardworking poor people around the country.

I'm with her because of them.

...watching her granddaughter have the opportunity she never had.

LAUREN, NEW YORK

The person I thought about more than anyone else

when I voted this year was my sister, Rachel. Born with a rare genetic disorder, she spent most of her life in a wheelchair. She was and is my hero. Tough as nails, a feminist, advocate, and writer. When Donald Trump mocked Serge Kovaleski, I pictured Rachel witnessing that. I was so upset, I couldn't think of much else for days. My vote is dedicated to my sister, Rachel, who is way too Nasty to *ever* Rest in Peace.

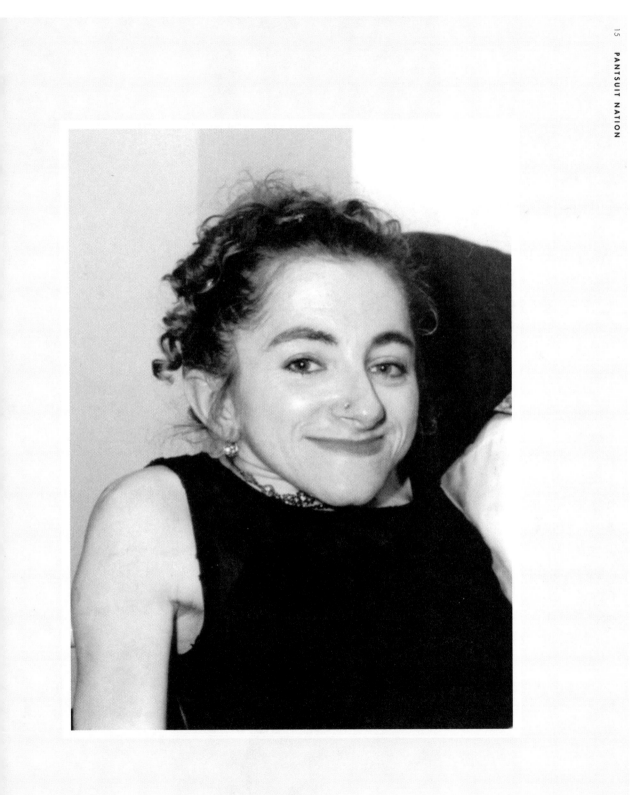

HILARY

This is me with my wife and family.

We created our family via fost-adopt and our beautiful boys are the lights of our lives. We will always be with her because her work to bring about the Adoption & Safe Families Act in 1997 has positively impacted our lives and directly contributed to our ability to create and support our family.

JACKIE, CALIFORNIA

My son is 8 years old.

He and his buddy from class decided, entirely on their own back in June, that they would vote for Hillary. I had to explain they would not be eligible until 2025, when both of her terms would be finished.

I am a first-generation Asian American. I could not be any prouder of my country, and I can't wait to hand over this great nation to my kid.

CHRISTINA, CALIFORNIA

I have always been an introvert.

I am quiet and deathly shy so public speaking and activism was never on the radar for me. I was a wallflower and content to stay that way. Following college, all I wanted to do was go back into the army. It was my first love, being part of something bigger than myself.

Unfortunately, that was taken away from me when someone outed me to the recruiter. It was 2008, so I interned for Clinton's campaign, as I believed she would be the candidate to repeal Don't Ask Don't Tell (DADT). I worked hard and walked many miles, knocking on doors and talking to voters in North Carolina. As a result of the work, I had the opportunity to meet Hillary. I have never been so terrified. I had brought my airborne wings, nothing shiny or new but my proudest possession, something I had to conquer a lot of fear and challenges to earn. As she approached to shake my hand, I handed her the wings and asked her to end DADT. She looked me in the eye and promised to do so. I had to convince her to take the wings, as I am sure she understood their significance.

Unfortunately, 2008 was not our year but I was struck by her hard work and determination. I got involved in the fight against DADT on a local level, lobbying congressional representatives for the cause. At one point, I was asked to speak at an event. I was terrified, definitely outside the comfort zone for an introvert. But I looked at Hillary's example. She had faced unending attacks but yet kept fighting for what she believed in. If she could do it, I could. So I spoke, I went to D.C. and lobbied. I did press interviews, received threats, but kept fighting on.

Here's the point. I am not voting for Hillary because I fear Trump. I am voting for her because she inspires me. I am who I am today because her example motivated me to get off my butt and fight for my rights. I may never see her again, but I am eternally grateful for that example and for that brief moment where she was so warm and compassionate.

> *I am who I am today because her example motivated me to get off my butt and fight for my rights.*

MICHAEL, TEXAS

I'd love to wear a pantsuit on Tuesday,

but as a lady trucker, that wouldn't be too practical! However, I'm a lifelong liberal Democrat and Afro-Latina

and although I will be on the road in any one of the lower forty-eight states on Tuesday, my absentee ballot has already been cast for Hillary.

ANTOINETTE, VIRGINIA

Our great-grandmother, grandmother, and cousins celebrating the women's right to vote!

I voted for them. For their future, their health care, their potential.

GRETCHEN, MASSACHUSETTS

For preexisting conditions. For mental health research funding. For her father and my love who we lost this summer after years of fighting for coverage and treatment.

We're with her.

This young man stood in line with me at age five to vote for Obama. It was a long line and as we made our way to the booth, Majin became visibly ill and I asked him if he wanted to sit down. He said, "No, this is too important. I will stand." Even at five he got what that election meant. At fourteen, he helped me knock on five hundred doors for Hillary! He knows how important this election is to our nation. Thus he will be in line witnessing history with me once again!

BERNADETTE EVANS & MAJIN LABRADOR, PENNSYLVANIA

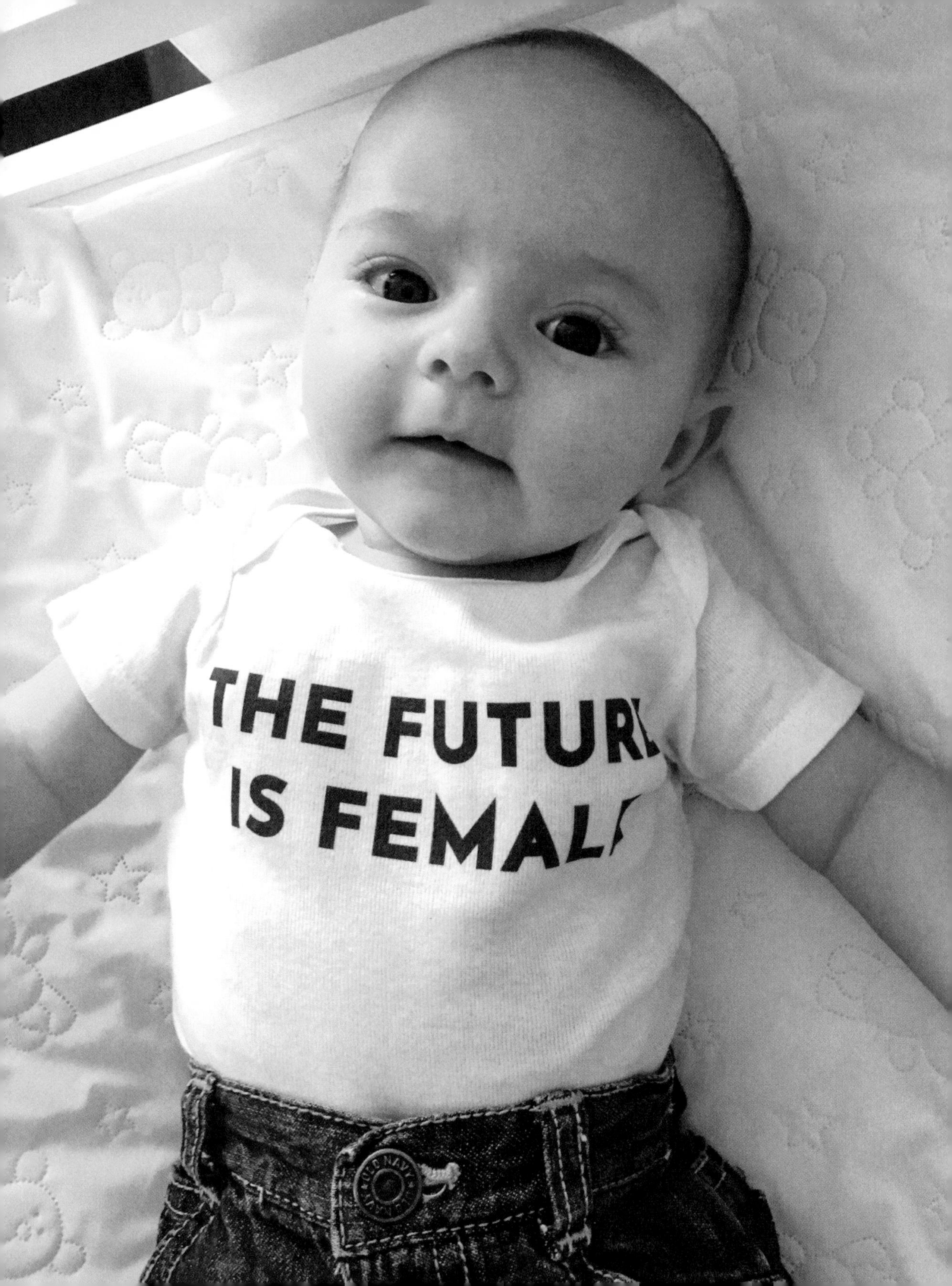
THE FUTUR
IS FEMAL

I'm voting for Hillary because I want my daughter to live in a world where sexual assault is not normalized, where racists, homophobes, and misogynists live in silent fear, and where feminist is not a dirty word.

REBECCA, RHODE ISLAND

We dropped off our ballot yesterday.

Even though we are in a solidly blue state, it felt great voting for Hillary and all that she represents. My daughter was super excited to help me fill in my ballot, as she has been Hillary's #1 fan since the beginning. I want to thank all of you for uplifting my spirits during the last couple of weeks. You helped remind me there are so many inspiring and dedicated people out there fighting the good fight.

SAL D., CALIFORNIA

My wife and I are with her

because she has promised to fight to ensure that people who identify as LGBTQIA will have full equality under the law and she will end the discrimination that happens within employment, housing, schools, and other aspects of our society.

AMANDA, TENNESSEE

My grandmother Henrietta, a.k.a. Hank, was a TWA airline stewardess in the 1930s,

It floored me. Blatant sexism oozes from every word. I started to understand the overwhelming forces she was pushing against.

when they were required to be registered nurses. On a flight one day, she was talking with a doctor/philanthropist from her hometown, Pittsburgh. She confided her dream to go to medical school, and he offered to sponsor her. He paid the tuition for her to attend Stanford Medical School, where she was the only woman in 1938. TWA used it as a publicity stunt and there were photos of her in papers across the country, both in her stewardess uniform and in a lab coat with a microscope. She arrived at school to bags of fan mail.

To pay the rest of her expenses, she worked nights as a nurse and acted as the live-in dorm mother for a house of undergraduates. None of her male classmates were holding down a second job, let alone two. She was so tired, she kept falling asleep in classes and labs. The letters from her sponsor are full of well-meaning but deeply patronizing advice.

She was also dating one of the glamorous pilots stationed at nearby Moffett Field. For

anymore. When the attacks came, she put it on, handed her baby to a neighbor, and went to work for three days. At one point, she convinced a soldier guarding a warehouse to look the other way while she broke in to steal blankets for the wounded.

She eventually had a second career as a science teacher for disadvantaged kids. She got me my first computer—a TRS-80 with 4K of memory—before anyone else had them. She was the only grandmother I knew who could stand on her head.

the end-of-year dinner at the dorm, it was her job to go buy the little gifts that were set at the places of every girl who had become engaged that year (!). My grandfather infamously proposed to her by mumbling, "You'd better get one more of those." She was so exhausted that she agreed.

The young couple was next stationed at Pearl Harbor, and my mother was a six-month-old baby on December 7, 1941. That day, my grandmother was laying out her nurse's uniform to send back to the States because she wasn't going to need it

For a long time, it was hard for me to understand why she quit and got married—quitting wasn't her style. Then one day I read the scrapbook she kept from her time at med school, including the news articles and letters. It floored me. Blatant sexism oozes from every word. I started to understand the overwhelming forces she was pushing against.

Today, I voted—for my daughter who loves science, for my single mother who had a career on Capitol Hill and fought for universal health care, and for my Grandma Retta. She would have made a heck of a doctor.

SUSAN, ONTARIO

Today, I wore my pantsuit for all my fellow Asian-American women who are anything but quiet, demure, and submissive.

I wore it for my grandma who immigrated to this country from the Philippines to create a better life for herself and her family. I wore it for my mom who works hard so that my brother and I can gain an education. I wore it for my friends and my generation for we are all still learning how to stand up and speak with conviction. I'm with her because she recognizes that our voices matter, and our America is one in which we have the chance to be heard.

This is the seventh cohort of the Asian-American Women's Political Initiative, the only program in the country designed to cultivate political leadership skills for Asian-American women.

ALEXIS, CALIFORNIA

Many people are concerned about millennial turnout for this election.

My name is Kristen, I'm African American and thirty years old. I'm voting for her because . . .

Black people were considered property, and were barely even considered humans, until 1865. I am voting for a candidate that understands my value to society and to the world. I'm voting for someone who won't implement policy that will very quickly take us back to one of the darkest times in our country's history—the Jim Crow era.

Although black men were granted the constitutional right to vote in 1870, they faced all *kinds* of intimidation, scare tactics, unfair taxes, and other measures—legal and illegal—to keep them from the polls. That all changed in 1965—that was only fifty years ago. Meaning, though it was legal,

> *We are stronger together than we are individually. America is a beautiful tapestry of ethnicities and religions. That is what makes this country great.*

people as young as my grandparents couldn't actually go to the polls and vote. Let that sink in.

I do not believe in socialism. I believe in giving a hand up, not a handout. I believe that, in times of need, it is not unreasonable to receive help. I am voting for a candidate who cares for and has a heart for people—not just the really wealthy white ones. I am voting for a candidate who cares for women and families and poverty and children.

There has *never* been anyone more qualified to hold this office. *Ever*. In the history of our country.

Every major genocide in the world has been preceded by classifying a group of people as "illegals." What happens next is they are considered to be threats and then become systematically eliminated. I will not stand by and let that happen again.

We are stronger together than we are individually. America is a beautiful tapestry of ethnicities and religions. *That* is what makes this country great. *I will not* support someone who cannot appreciate all of our differences.

As a Christian, I will *not* vote for a homophobic, xenophobic, misogynistic, nationalistic, racist bigot who is *incapable* of bringing people together, *refuses* to work across party lines, and does not understand that you do not lead by inciting violence and perpetuating fear.

Lastly, I'm with her because I already voted last Monday. No going back now!

KRISTEN, TEXAS

I wish you could see my whole shirt. Fighting cancer and fighting for Hillary.

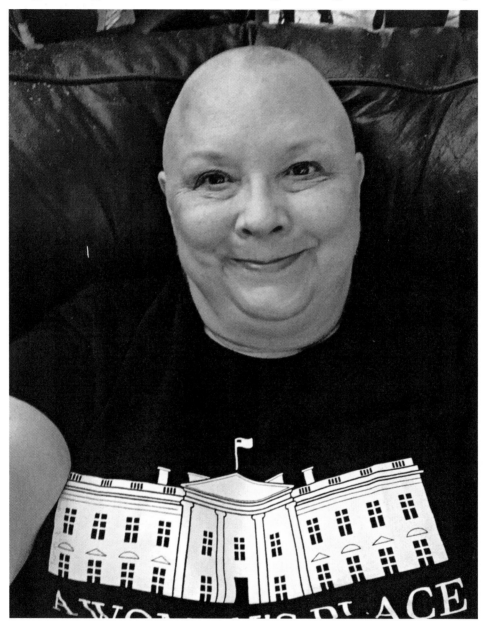

PAM, ALABAMA

I've been a staunch Hillary Clinton supporter since she fought for health care reform the first time she was in the White House, when she campaigned against then Senator Obama in 2007, and even more so now that she is *the* most qualified presidential candidate ever in our nation's history. So yes, from a ranch owner from Texas, **I'm with her!**

JONATHAN, TEXAS

When Trump talks about building walls

and banning people from other countries, I think of my husband, Yandy, a man that never took things for granted. A man who works very hard and has a dream to be an engineer one day. I am so proud and love him so much, I also know he is just as proud to be an American. I love this country for giving him the opportunities which otherwise would never happen in Cuba.

These stories are many and true for immigrants looking to live a better life. My father told me he had escaped to Hong Kong by swimming across shark-infested waters during China's communist rule before emigrating to America. There are many stories that I have heard that would put tears in your eyes and break your heart. For us who were born here in America, we can't even comprehend the horror some immigrants went through in their country to get here.

We got married last year and this is the first year my husband is able to vote since becoming a US citizen. We are happy and hopeful for our future. We know we still have a lot of work to do and we will do it together.

> *We can't even comprehend the horror some immigrants went through in their country to get here.*

ALBERT, FLORIDA

We're with her!

AMY, JANET & NICOLE, GEORGIA

HIS FAVORITE HAT

MASHEED ROCKWELL, SOUTH CAROLINA

I'm twenty-four years old, and last week, I voted early in New Orleans.

I'm the daughter of Cuban immigrants and my family fled Cuba having only ever dreamt of being able to live in a country where they could vote again. I was born in the US and am forever grateful for their sacrifice.

I live in the heart of the South and I'm a brown queer woman which some days feels like a blessing and some days feels like a burden. I work in the nonprofit sector and I teach part-time as a high school Spanish teacher at a school that is 90 percent black. I also spent a year working at my local public defender's office as a client advocate and interpreter. I say all of this because these experiences have shaped me and shape who

I vote for. I know that my vote is more than just *my* vote. My vote has so much to do with intersectionality. When I was at the polls, I thought about which candidate is pro-immigration and pro-refugee. I thought about which candidate had undocumented individuals on the convention stage and portrayed them in a positive light. I thought about which candidate is pro-woman. I thought about which candidate realizes that the criminal justice system is broken and mass incarceration is tearing families apart. I thought about which candidate has said that Black Lives Matter. I thought about which candidate believes in marriage equality and will advocate on other LGBTQIA issues like trans rights.

When I cast my vote last week, it was a vote that had the weight of those who are unable to vote because they are either undocumented or because they are in jail / on probation or parole / have felony convictions (over 6 million individuals). It was also a vote for the tens of thousands who have lost their lives to suicide (or hate crimes) based on their mental health issues, bullying, etc., stemming from their gender identity or sexual orientation. My vote isn't just a vote for me but a vote for them. It's a vote for us.

In the last five years, I've been called everything under the sun. I've been called a spic, a f*g, a dyke, a beaner, a wetback, a bulldagger, and more. I've been told to go back to my country or to go jump off a bridge because I'm disgusting and perverse.

Well, guess what? I'm proud, I'm brown, I'm queer, I'm still here, and I'm with her.

ILEANA, LOUISIANA

My vote isn't just a vote for me but a vote for them. It's a vote for us.

I never want another person with a disability to experience being told they aren't smart enough to pursue their dreams in employment, just so the employer can pay them less than minimum wage.

Tomorrow, though I may not physically be able to wear a pantsuit,

I will cast my vote for HRC proudly knowing that she has put the needs of the disabled as one of her top priorities. I never want another person with a disability to experience being told they aren't smart enough to pursue their dreams in employment, just so the employer can pay them less than minimum wage.

After high school, I went into a rehab facility that promised me the ability to get physical therapy and further my education with college classes after an evaluation assessment for employment. I was determined to work in the computer field, but wasn't sure in what aspect. While in high school I had taken a year of college-level accounting, maintaining solid As. Imagine my shock when after their evaluation they told me I wasn't smart enough to do computer work of *any* kind, but they would gladly help me become a CPA! Accounting bored me to death but since it was all they would pay for . . . okay. Every day I was turning in work ahead of time, acing it all, and being asked by the professor why I was in his class since I knew all the material. This lasted four months and then I quit.

To make a very long story a bit shorter, I got an old computer, taught myself DOS, read every book I could get my hands on about computers, and finally (with assistance through the Department of Rehabilitative Services) got into classes through my local community college. I became a graphic design expert and ran my own business for ten years, all while raising my son and taking care of my husband (something else I wasn't supposed to be able to do).

Tomorrow is important to us all, but especially if you are disabled! This is my picture to show the level of my (so-called) disability.

LYNN ORANGE, VIRGINIA

My ninety-three-year-old mom, Jewel, is with Hillary!

How important is this election?

Every vote is so critical that my seventy-two-year-old grandmother voted for the first time!

She's been a citizen for nearly two decades. She spent most of that time living with her husband in California. He has since passed away so she moved back home this spring to be with my parents.

While visiting home last week I asked her if she was voting. "I've never voted," she told me.

I was stunned.

She went on to say that no one has ever asked if she wanted to vote. She was worried about not knowing English. She didn't know how to register. She didn't know where to vote.

But guess what? She knew more about the candidates than most people I've talked to. In fact, my mom asked a question about the candidates and my grandma surprised us by spitting out the facts. I asked her how she learned it all. "I listen to Hmong radio," she said.

Needless to say, my siblings got her registered. She cast her ballot last Friday. She was so happy she finally got to exercise her right as an American.

BOUA XIONG-ROY, MINNESOTA

Drugged and
gang-raped
twenty-plus
years ago by a
roomful of young
men who had
clearly been
raised to believe
it was theirs for
the taking.
Got 'er done
today, for my
daughters
and yours.

JENNY

My "pantsuit" was the uniform I wore for three years,

serving my country. In 1964 we US Navy women didn't have much of a pantsuit to wear (except dark blue dungarees and a chambray shirt when working). I've been wearing an invisible pantsuit all my life. I grew up in the 1960s and embraced the rise of feminism and supported civil rights.

My mother, Ruth May Zimmerman, was in Hawaii and worked for the US Navy on Ford Island in civil service. She experienced the attack on Pearl Harbor just as my father, Jack Zimmerman, US Navy pharmacist's mate first class, did. He was at the Honolulu hospital working like all the others did, to help the wounded from that attack. My mother woke up that morning because a Japanese Zero flew down her street, spraying bullets into all the houses. She had a bullet hit just above the headboard of her bed and go through the other wall.

I come from a military family on both sides of my family. I served because I love my country. We are all Americans, not a party. We need to be *in*clusive, not *ex*clusive.

I'm seventy now, but that doesn't stop me in the least from continuing to champion women's rights, the rights of *all* people not to be classified or excluded because of their race, religion, or gender. I've devoted my life to championing the cause of women in the military being respected and treated as equals. When I was in during the Vietnam War, I was sexually harassed every day, no matter where I went on base.

Women are so much stronger than any man. We know how to network, to work as a *team*. Let's keep doing it! For the good of *all*.

I've been wearing an invisible pantsuit all my life.

R. E. NAUMAN, ARIZONA

I've decided to take my six-year-old granddaughter with me to vote on Tuesday. It just occurred to me that I want to share this important, historical process with her. I feel slightly emotional when I consider all this could mean for her future.

Pantsuit activated.

LOLA, OKLAHOMA

First time voting! I was not going to apply for my citizenship until the sad episode of "they steal our jobs ..." As a Peruvian immigrant, I am not going to give up on this country, not to people like Trump. I will keep fighting and I hope people will open their eyes and not follow the path of the ignorance and hate.

CLAUDIA HOLZBAUER, MINNESOTA

I'm with her because I want my four young daughters to not come home from school in fear that they are not going to be allowed to stay in the United States because their mom wasn't born here and that's what their friends are telling them at school.

I'm with her because I want them to always know that they are the ones who are able to make their own decisions about their bodies.

Their bodies, their choices.

I'm with her because I want them to always be kind and respectful and loving of all people regardless of race, religion, sexual orientation, and everything in between.

I'm with her because she is the only choice that makes sense. I'm with her because she is going to be the best choice for my girls' future.

ANNA ALLEN, OHIO

VOTE →

FIRST-
TIME
VOTER
↘

SHERRILYN, SOUTH CAROLINA

It's a beautiful day for a **Nasty Woman,** for her fierce two-year-old daughter, and for her three-year-old little boy with a disability. I'm so with her.

ROSEANNE, NEW YORK

I am still gathering my pantsuit for tomorrow

but I have to say as a Nez Perce Tribal Member and African-American woman from the Northwest, I am very proud to vote for Hillary Clinton. I keep thinking about all the wonderful things my mom, who is sixty-seven, and my gram, who is ninety, have passed down to me: family, personal independence, being mindful and active in regard to environmental issues, love, loyalty, human rights issues, sticking up for the underdog, standing up for myself, and retaining my heritage despite living in a Western world.

Some of us were already here in the US and we are not all immigrants. My dad's side is from Nashville, originally from Cheap Hill, Tennessee, a former plantation, and we were former slaves. Progress is imperative and my Granny said when President Obama was elected, "I never thought I'd see it in my lifetime," and she's ninety-seven!

I posed a question to my family on what they thought about Hillary becoming president. The consensus was *it's about time* to have a woman in the White House. My hope is that she continues the work laid by her predecessors and President Obama in regards to social issues, human rights, families, women and children, Indigenous Peoples, LGBTQIA rights, upholding *Roe v. Wade*, and the progression of the great work that Planned Parenthood continues to do.

This is not just about Democrats winning, it's about moving forward with *all of us in mind*. It's complicated, it's diverse, but we're all here together.

My vote is for my nine-year-old boy, my twenty-five-year-old daughter, and my four-year-old granddaughter, i.e.: The Future.

DEANNA, WASHINGTON

It's complicated, it's diverse, but we're all here together.

This is my grandmother,

whom I never got to meet because she died after having an abortion during the Depression, leaving three small children. Of course, abortions were illegal then and she had to go to someone who wasn't licensed.

I'm with her because I do not want to go back to the Dark Ages. I voted in her memory. Let's go forward and continue to support and love one another because we're better together!

DEBORAH LEOCI MEISENBERG, FLORIDA

I'm with her.

I'm with her. I'm with her.

I do it for my mom (1962–2015), who was raped in her twenties, suffered from debilitating depression, and was despised by many of her family members for going against the grain. She was my hero and she would have voted for Hillary as many times as she possibly could.

I do it for my wife of nine years, who is in the midst of transitioning genders, but who has still managed to lead a tech company with grace and humility.

I do it for our unborn children, who will live in a world with two moms, children we want to feel safe and loved.

It is my belief that the breaking of this glass ceiling will open the floodgates for women in the US. It will inspire generations. It will lead to more thoughtful and loving discourse in politics. We will evolve.

We will. We will. We will.

She is us and we are her.

ASHLEY, NEVADA

July 22, 2016, was the day we were supposed to be married.

Instead, my husband began chemotherapy to treat his aggressive lymphoma. We were married in a hospital room at Swedish First Hill in Seattle. His battle continues over four months later. We're with her because she supports marriage equality and nondiscrimination. We're with her because our marriage allows me to use sick leave and FMLA to care for my husband. We're with her because Hillary supports health care that does not recognize preexisting conditions.

Update: David lost his long and courageous battle on November 19, 2016, with me by his side.

SEAN & DAVID, WASHINGTON

This pantsuit-wearing silent majority looks forward to having a seat at the table. Let's break that glass ceiling! **We can do it!**

LEIAH ROBBINS, CALIFORNIA

My father served thirty years. I am a disabled Afghanistan veteran and former paratrooper. My husband serves, and our child is a military brat. I'm with her because she stands with our military members and our military families.

MEGAN, HAWAII

My grandmother, much like Hillary's mother, had a very hard life.

She lived in Shanghai during World War II and the civil war. Bombers and fighter jets would fly overhead while she was raising four boys on her own in a small apartment with no toilet and a shared coal-fired kitchen. Her husband lived thousands of miles away, earning money in Hong Kong. She also suffered from tuberculosis, but never stopped volunteering for her community and did everything she could to help her boys have a better future.

Years later she moved to New York City and lived in Manhattan's Chinatown with my grandfather. They watched the World Trade Center fall from their kitchen window on 9/11. In the weeks following, with an air purifier delivered to them largely due to Hillary's advocacy for public health protections for the people of New York, my grandparents draped their apartment in American flags and memorabilia, much like the rest of the city's residents. I don't get patriotic when I think about the wars that America has fought and won. I get patriotic when I think of that New York Chinatown apartment, and how immigrants who barely spoke English could feel such profound allegiance to their country. That is what makes America a truly special place. That my grandparents didn't have to give up their

I don't get patriotic when I think about the wars that America has fought and won. I get patriotic when I think of that New York Chinatown apartment, and how immigrants who barely spoke English could feel such profound allegiance to their country.

identities to become American. They could live perfectly comfortably in New York City, go to the pharmacy, buy newspapers, do their banking, and start and run businesses in this country that afforded them and their children safety, economic and educational opportunities, and clean air to breathe.

I now live in Seattle, raising two boys as a middle-class working mom in a city with rapidly rising housing prices, expensive child care, and a spotty public education system. Whenever I think I'm having a hard day, I think about my grandmother and how much worse it could be. I know that Hillary seeks that same mentality—of checking one's privilege. This "get shit done" attitude is uniquely born out of adversity, family, and hard work. I believe that America's diverse experiences are what give us strength; immigrants are not a weakness.

SIAN, WASHINGTON

In 2012, my family members became US citizens to vote for Obama. **This year, I became a US citizen to vote for Hillary Clinton and help make history as a woman, as an immigrant, and as a Latina. Tomorrow, history will be made!**

CRISTINA, ARIZONA

Women for H

Text WOMEN to 47246*

I'M WITH HER

On November 8, more than 120,000 members posted to Pantsuit Nation, including tens of thousands of pantsuit and voting selfies.

Love trumps hate.

VOTED

Dear Pantsuit Nation

(have you ever heard a better name?!),

On this historic day, I wanted to take a moment to thank you for your support from the bottom of my heart.

This election hasn't been easy: It's been long, hard-fought, and at times it made us question who we are as Americans. For some of you, it's been difficult to feel like you could wear your support on your sleeve—and that's why this community has been such a special place. Your stories and photos of family members and friends are wonderful to see, but what truly warms my heart is the thousands of comments of support and love you all send to each other. I'm honored and humbled to have all of you with me, but I'm even prouder to see this community represent the best of America: people of all backgrounds and beliefs who share a vision for a brighter future for our children, and who have each other's backs. That's who we really are, and tonight, we're going to prove it.

Thank you all so much for your support, your hard work, and your votes. Tonight, I hope we'll finally break through that highest, hardest glass ceiling together, and use those pantsuits for the best occasion of all—celebrating!

HILLARY RODHAM CLINTON

ELECTORAL

65,844,610

62,979,636

POPULAR

H
E
R

Today has been hard.

Like so many of you, I had been looking forward to the morning of November 9, 2016, for a long, long time. But instead of excitement and relief, I have been mired in disbelief, sadness, fear, and heartache for much of the day.

But there are 3.1 million glimmers out there tonight. I know you are all hurting, but you're still glowing. This is our hope, pantsuiters. This group—our shared positivity and love and strength—has made a difference these last three weeks. And this is just the beginning. Pantsuit Nation is *more* important today than it was yesterday. Secretary Clinton called on us in her incredible, gracious speech this morning. We need to make our voices heard.

LIBBY CHAMBERLAIN, MAINE

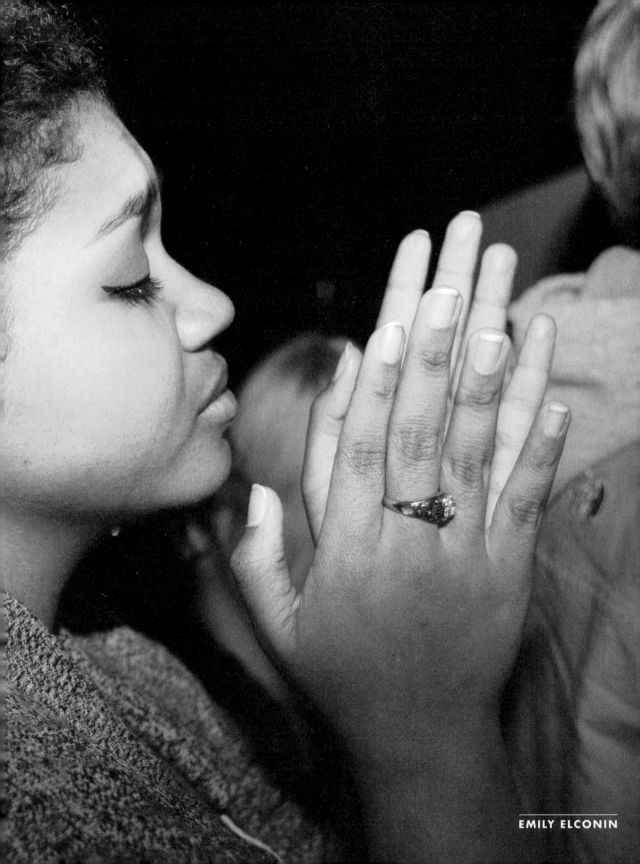

Waking up to
this nightmare
in Stockholm.

Trying not to let
my children see
how scared I am.

Love will
always win.

We just
have to
believe
that.

For our
kids.

Despite this horrific turn of events I promise to continue.

I will continue to stand up for what I believe in and fight for what is right.

I will continue to serve my nation for the citizens who are currently in despair.

I will continue to be a soldier for the young LGBTQIA citizens who also dream to wear the uniform.

I will continue to be a role model of tolerance, empathy, and equality.

I will continue to educate myself and others on the minorities in our country who need support.

I will continue to fight for my fellow women to ensure our personal rights and safety.

I will continue to be the voice of reason for those in need and I will never give up on any of them.

I still feel the embarrassment and the shame of our country's decision but I am still an American. I will not abandon that and flee to Canada or Switzerland because America needs people like me to continue to stand up for those who don't have the luxury to just move away.

I will be the change I want to see in our nation.

LEA, WASHINGTON

I am fired up, ready to go!

Last night, I cried.

I went to bed mourning the nation that I imagined to exist. This morning, I am no longer crying. That nation *does* exist. I am listening, especially to the genuine fear and worry that lies beneath the hateful language and the lashing out. I am learning. I am thinking about the interplay of justice, freedom, and opportunity. I am fired up, ready to go! The community represented by Pantsuit Nation is inspiring, positive, hopeful. There is an amazing amount of love and caring here for each other, for the nation, and for the planet. We just need to harness this energy!

NAAMAL, DISTRICT OF COLUMBIA

Madame Secretary, thank you for bringing us closer to breaking that glass ceiling!

My sweet four-year-old woke up this morning and said, "Mom, I want to send Hillary a card. She's probably sad like us." She wrote it all herself, and we mailed it together. I'm so proud that even at four she sees the injustice, but stays positive and just wants to spread love.

ANONYMOUS

Two years ago today,

Mariam Khan and I got married. Today, I am prouder than ever to be a Jewish American married to a Muslim American.

Shortly after our wedding, we moved to New York so I could join Hillary's campaign. Though working for twenty-two months with a grueling campaign schedule wasn't the ideal way most couples start their marriage, we were committed to fight for what we believe in.

While we didn't get the outcome we wanted on Election Day, as we celebrate our anniversary, we are reminded that love trumps hate

We're still ready to fight for what is right and know that we are always stronger together.

DAVID, NEW YORK

The heart of America can't be captured in memes or ad campaigns.

Mel was an Ohio transplant

wrapping up a master's degree in Waco when we met just shy of five years ago. He was playing saxophone in a Pink Floyd cover band at the bar where a friend had convinced me to humor him by coming along as a young student myself, a gay man, and a devout homebody. Meeting him has become the biggest adventure of my life.

We have struggled together as broke college students and celebrated together when we purchased our first home. We have struggled as individuals in doing our best to show up for one another despite ourselves. This is the America we long and fight for every day.

This is our little piece of America that has been humbled by this election. I'm grateful for the outgoing administration and its ambition for the minority. An administration that invigorated communities who were hungry for wind in their sails. This election felt personal for millions of Americans. We all see it, and we will likely see it for some time to come. Denying that is counterproductive to a unified America. So, I guess this post is about visibility, hope, and optimism going forward.

The heart of America can't be captured in memes or ad campaigns. It's going to take heart. We have to contribute stories in the hope that they will begin to merge with those we aren't familiar with.

NICK, TEXAS

This is my ♥.

Garrett. A person. My smile. My music. My reason. Not a drain on the economy or the health care system. And *certainly* not someone who deserves a president who will mock him or those like him. Thank you all for standing with us. You give us hope.

BONNIE LAPEÉ, MISSOURI

I have a nine-year-old and a six-month-old. The *only* president my nine-year-old has ever known is someone who looks just like him. A fair and honest man who only tries to do what's best for all people. The first president my six-month-old will ever know is Donald Trump. The disparity is so vast. How is that fair? Prayers for us all.

SAKENA, NORTH CAROLINA

I was terrified

when I painted my fence, and terrified all last week. I bought these colors on Wednesday morning and had a bad experience with some customers at Home Depot when I bought them. Then I lay in bed all week crying and planning my escape to Canada. I'm a thirty-seven-year-old trans woman who just moved back to my college town.

And then *boom*—Donald Trump is president.

I went through periods of vicious anger this week. I was talking to my closest friends and saying we should maybe launch a revolution. And I cried and thought about just drowning myself in the bathtub.

It's been a rough week. But seeing everyone happy about my fence cemented the feeling I got from my local liberal community outreach/organizer friend. We're going to fight this wave of anger and hate not with more anger and hate but with good deeds and standing up proudly. Because if someone doesn't want me around, I'm going to make it clear why. Because I am going to be *so damn nice* and *kind* and *good* over the next four years that nobody will be able to blame people like me for anything in four years. They'll be too busy thanking me for the biscuits and casseroles I make them. Thanking me for fixing their fences and

continued...

Because I am going to be *so damn nice* and *kind* and *good* over the next four years that nobody will be able to blame people like me for anything in four years.

mowing their lawns. Since Sunday morning I have met someone who lives at every one of the houses on my two-block street. I have told them all I am "queer as a three-dollar bill and an atheist and a great neighbor." They have all agreed that I am a good person and I agreed that they are too. I have fixed a neighbor's fence. Traded numbers with as many people as possible, and made homemade biscuits for everyone I met.

I also want to extend the olive branch to all of you. I am in Missouri. This state was never in play. I'm going to be honest and say I sat down at my polling place and voted for "Steve 'Captain America' Rogers" while crying my eyes out. Because I believe it's going to take a miracle to save us all. And that miracle is you and me and your neighbor getting up early and using good deeds to show the other side that we are all good people who are all scared for what the future will bring. Let's work together and let's all be friends—even with people who hate our guts. I love you. I will help you fix your problems and I will be a good neighbor.

BETHANY, MISSOURI

When I came home tonight, my husband said, "I have a surprise for you. Since Trump has won, I've decided it was time to show my values." He said he knew how sad I've been feeling and wanted to make me smile. This man went on a feminist website to order himself two feminist T-shirts!

EMILY, DISTRICT OF COLUMBIA

My sweet daughter was the youngest volunteer

for Hillary in Raleigh, North Carolina. She was ecstatic about helping people with disabilities to their seats before Michelle Obama's speech, because she has a special-needs sister and it made her feel good to help others. How lucky she was to hear the words Michelle spoke. She talked about the experience for weeks. Glad she will carry this memory for all of her days and remember that women *do* have a voice.

LILY, NORTH CAROLINA

These are my kids. All four of them. My husband is Filipino. Our oldest is adopted (domestic), and our other three are biological and half Asian. We have had a lot of tough conversations this past week. Not just about what will likely be said to us but how to respond and get help for themselves or to protect a friend or stranger. We've experienced racism before, it comes with the territory. We are beautifully diverse and I wouldn't change a single thing. We will get through this, I know.

SARAH, INDIANA

It was the day after the Supreme Court ruled on marriage. The three of us were running errands at our local hardware store and a shopper walked up to us and said, "Congratulations, I am a supporter! Can I please give you all a hug?" We all embraced, with tears in our eyes. I will always remember that moment. There has always been *goodness* in this country. That is what we teach our son and what will keep us going.

HERB, FLORIDA

LOVE IS LOVE
BLACK LIVES MATTER
CLIMATE CHANGE IS
IMMIGRANTS MAKE
WOMEN'S RIGHTS ARE

A GREAT

UMAN RIGHTS

JAMIE THROWER, CALIFORNIA

This is my thirteen-year-old daughter, Molly.

She has Rett syndrome, a neurological disorder that affects one in ten thousand *girls* and *women* worldwide. Molly cannot walk or talk and often has uncontrolled hand movements much like the ones Donald Trump made fun of and mocked in reporter Serge Kovaleski. I have watched, often silently, as my daughter is stared at. I have watched as people have pointed and spoken in hushed whispers, "What is wrong with her?" I have spent tireless hours educating others on disability and acceptance, and my fears now have become a hard reality.

Not only does my family face catastrophic cuts to the social service programs that allow us to care for her at home but I fear that the walls to tolerance and acceptance which we have worked so hard to chip away at are being slowly built back up. How long before children think it is okay to mock, ignore, and marginalize her? How long before she realizes that she is not a valued member of our society? Here is my plea. If you see a disabled child, please, speak to them, smile at them, let their parents know that you are committed to taking care of the most vulnerable members of our society.

I fear that the walls to tolerance and acceptance which we have worked so hard to chip away at are being slowly built back up.

LAUREN, DISTRICT OF COLUMBIA

Pantsuit Nation, I witnessed today the union between a West African Muslim immigrant and a Christian American woman. I look around this beautiful room and see people from different races, cultures, and religions dance, rejoice, and celebrate together. My spirit is lifted! No more fear! Love trumps hate.

FATIMA FALL, CALIFORNIA

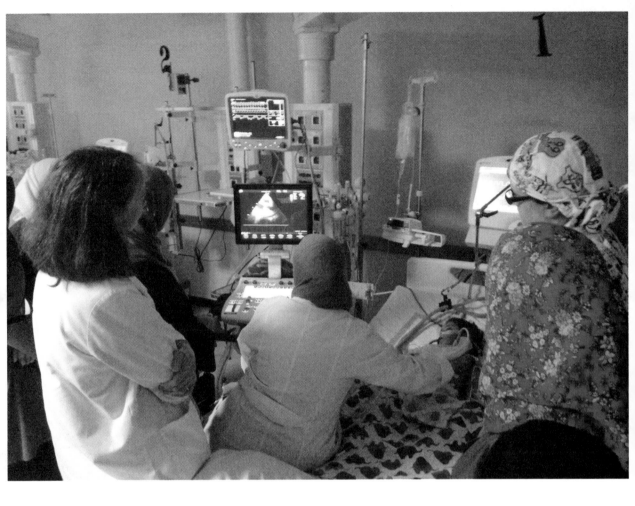

Stereotypes are a funny thing.

A few days ago in our ICU in Benghazi, Libya (yup, *that* Benghazi), we had a team conference about a sick little patient. Two Libyan cardiologists and the local pediatric heart surgeon consulted with the ICU doctor, nurses, and surgeon from my medical NGO.

We are all women.

Between us we are Libyan, Palestinian, Belorussian, Australian, and from the USA. Muslim, Christian, atheist.

Working together. For one child.

LIBBY SAUTER, NEVADA

Josh and I would like to thank everyone from Pantsuit Nation

who came to Central Park yesterday to celebrate our marriage as well as the multitude of well-wishers who sent their love from every corner of this nation and beyond. I never knew what my wedding day would be like but there was something so magical about being surrounded by such a diverse group of close friends and new friends all united by the same desire to spread love during a divided, shattered time. For the first moment since Tuesday night, I woke up beaming and I think I'm finally ready to activate and start making changes.

My deepest thanks to Karen, who saw the post on Pantsuit Nation and offered to be our impromptu wedding photographer.

Rose and Julia were among those Pantsuit Nation members who attended. They made a beautiful heartfelt sign for us. I'll treasure it always. And there were many more who showed up. You all made an imprint on my heart.

As I begin this new chapter with my husband by my side, I hope we all remember that love will always win. Hillary's message lives on loud and clear: "Do all the good you can, for all the people you can, in all the ways you can, as long as ever you can."

JESSE & JOSH, NEW YORK

As the grandmother of three biracial children

(two who are alive, and one who passed away after a courageous battle against congenital heart disease), I struggle with the handful of friends and extended family members who voted for Trump. Those same people who stood by my family's side during my grandson's six-month stay in the cardiac ICU, who donated to heart charities, who sent flowers and cards to his memorial service, who prayed for him to live, have sent me a loud and clear message that black lives don't matter. That my family doesn't matter. That, had my grandson lived to see his teen years, he could have been killed in an instant as a result of "stop and frisk" and the militarization of the police force that Trump supports. Their votes told me that they would support the elimination of Obamacare while knowing that my family would have been in financial ruin if we had to pay the more than $2 million in hospital bills. I can't wrap my head around the fact that these people can't see that they voted against my family. I can't watch them "like" pictures that my African-American daughters post of my two surviving grandchildren without wanting to scream that you don't get to have it both ways. You don't get to vote for Trump and then profess to care about my family.

Update: To everyone here, thank you for your kind words, for your compassion, for your empathy, and most of all, for your solidarity. I can't even begin to express how much I appreciate each and every one of you! Please know that I, and everyone in my immediate family, stands with everyone here who has been hurt and victimized by this election (people of color, immigrants, refugees, the LGBTQIA community, people who are differently abled, women, survivors of sexual assault, and families who suffer from catastrophic illnesses).

My personal story

of being a woman of color.

I used to be ashamed of the color of my skin. I didn't see women of color on the covers of magazines, nor see them as Barbie dolls. I remember like it was yesterday the first time I received a racist comment. I was about thirteen years old, I played for hours in the sun as my skin turned to a roasted, dark coffee color. I was swinging high in the clouds at the playground. Not a worry in the world. Slowly, the swing made smaller trips to the sky, and eventually back to the ground. I looked up to see kids sliding down. A boy at the top of the play structure, no older than ten, yelled, "Go back to Mexico where you belong!" My face turned red. My heart sunk to my belly. And I yelled. I can't remember what I yelled, but I stormed off. And never told anyone. Until now.

That day, I looked in the mirror and looked at my skin. I was uncomfortable. Young, hurt, and naïve, I placed Desitin on my face, that thick, white lotion made to get rid of rashes, hoping it would change the color of my skin. I tried hiding from the sun, so my skin wouldn't be so dark.

I was no longer an innocent child stuck in the clouds—that swing had to eventually drop to reality. I came to realize that society sees me differently.

So when people say "stop whining" about the recent election, or "my vote for Trump does not represent my true values," they really don't understand the big picture. I fear for my brothers and sisters, who have faced unfair judgments according to their skin color and not their character. No, I was not being a sore loser when I was mourning Hillary's loss. I was mourning for the people who are treated unfairly based on their income, documents, skin, identity, religion, gender, and for the safety of Mother Earth.

Now, at twenty-six, I love my skin, I am proud to be Latina. So dang proud. I know there are young children who may be wearing my old shoes. So please, remember to check in with your children/students and do not be afraid to have honest, uncomfortable conversations about race, religion, gender, etc. I'm a firm believer in sustainable change, which must begin with our youth. They are our future. Let's teach them inclusiveness and to love each other and themselves. I share my story, to be vulnerable, and maybe let someone else know they are not alone. I'm fired up to be an advocate for you all.

> *I was no longer an innocent child stuck in the clouds—that swing had to eventually drop to reality. I came to realize that society sees me differently.*

ELISABET, WASHINGTON

I am the granddaughter of two Holocaust survivors

who beat unthinkable odds and survived multiple concentration camps, unlike their countless relatives who weren't quite so lucky. They met wandering around the ashes of postwar Poland, had my mother in a DP camp in Germany, and emigrated to the US shortly thereafter. They went on to build a good life and community for themselves here in this country. But the scars of the Holocaust always remained in my family, just as the tattoos remained burned on their arms.

I cannot express to you the uneasiness, the fear I feel as a third-generation survivor when I hear the hateful speech of Donald Trump as well as his supporters and advisors. I am grateful that my grandparents were not around to see a demagogue rise to power this year, along with a culture of normalized anti-Semitism, racism, xenophobia, sexism, and homophobia.

As someone who comes from a family who were victims of bigotry, and as a compassionate person with friends of many colors, religious backgrounds, and orientations, I am concerned about the hateful atmosphere that now pervades in this country. This tenor is the result of Trump's rhetoric, and will only become more pervasive—perhaps even cemented in legislature—if we stand by and allow dangerous appointments to his cabinet. White supremacists like Steve Bannon and Jeff Sessions have no place in our government. Do we really want to be a nation in which the leader of the Ku Klux Klan endorses a president's cabinet picks and policies?

LAUREN, NEW YORK

This is me, Vince, and my hubb'n, Chuck.

We've been together for twelve years and married for eight. Yay! From Georgia, we flew to San Diego and married just before Prop 8 shut down gay marriage in California. It was, at the time, one place where we didn't have to lie about our intentions just to get married. Some requirements outside of California, like Massachusetts, wanted it in writing that we intended to move there. Nothing against Massachusetts but we are Southern boys, and in spite of all the pitfalls that comes with that, it's still our home. Though we are so very proud to have been counted as part of the eighteen thousand that got married in California during that very brief moment in 2008, we are even more proud to see the few, albeit small, steps our state has taken toward equality for all. But what seemed impossible

when I was young and gay here is now legal. What a rush! We almost went blue this year and we're optimistic that one day we will.

There will always be challenges to face and improvements to make. We're human and we're messy. But as Obama pointed out, progress doesn't move in a straight line. Progress in the gay community has often felt like a roller coaster. And while it's easy to become self-absorbed in our own personal challenges and journeys, we must remind ourselves that others hurt too and that together we can overcome anything. To everyone in Pantsuit Nation, keep the faith, stay alert, strong, safe, and above all else, accepting of *everyone*. It's not just a movement, it's who we are. We're Americans.

It's not just a movement, it's who we are.

My nine-year-old daughter battled brain cancer for almost a year. She passed away October 26. Prior to that we spent nearly a month at St. Jude in Memphis and we had the opportunity to spend a great deal of quality time together and had quite a few discussions about the upcoming election. She told me, "Mom, if I could vote I would vote for Hillary Clinton." When I asked her why, she told me she liked what she had to say and she felt that Trump was a bully on top of it. Amelia was all about kindness, and through her almost yearlong battle, I refused to give up on her, and now I refuse to give up on kindness.

JILL, MISSOURI

ROBIN SEWELL DAUM

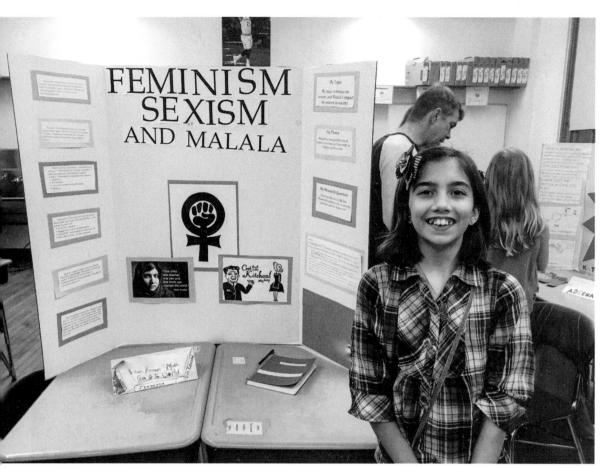

I was greatly heartened yesterday as I went to my daughter's school presentation night. She had chosen a very relevant topic to our time, but she was not alone. I listened to child after child give eloquent presentations on religious tolerance, clean energy, recycling, medical rights of minors, and many more. The world is a scary place right now, but I was nearly brought to tears by these smart, passionate, informed twelve-year-olds.

GINA, OHIO

Hi, my name is Saadia.

I'm twenty-five, I have a disability called cerebral palsy, I'm a lesbian, and I'm black. Let's remember to be kind to one another and be there for each other no matter what it is. Just because Trump is president now doesn't mean my personality will change. I'm still Saadia at the end of the day and you're still you. We'll get through this together.

Trudy and I would have been married three years today.

We spent nearly fifteen years together. Trudy used to say, "We're married, we're just not churched." That makes me smile, even now. In the end, we didn't get churched at all, though I'd argue that God was certainly present—we were married in a small civil ceremony in Lewiston, New York.

We were married for seven months. Cancer took that away from us.

Cancer had, in fact, been the impetus for our marriage. It became, in so many ways, more urgent for us to make it official—emotionally certainly, and practically—my employer had (at long last) stepped up and expanded the definition of spouse to the broadest possible application, allowing for Trudy to be on my medical plan.

I will ever be grateful for that action. I am grateful, too, for the actions of the Obama administration in setting the country on a course toward marriage equality. I am perhaps less grateful for the fractious set of barriers that came later; married in one state that embraced marriage equality, residing in another state that did not; recognized as married federally, not recognized at the

But that status became like a badge of honor to me. One I certainly never wanted, but nonetheless, I wore it like a crown.

state level; filing taxes federally as married; refiling as single for state taxes. It seems a needlessly complex system.

And then, Trudy died. My heart broke and my sense of self forever changed at that exact moment and no words can satisfactorily define the experience so I shall not try—but it was, if you'll forgive me for putting it this way, an interesting time (in our nation's history) to die, especially for a married lesbian.

I am ever grateful that we had the presence of mind and the forethought to put all of our documents in order—our will, our powers of attorney—we even had a partnership agreement in place in the event, as Trudy liked to say, "I ever left her for a younger woman." (smile)

But it was not easy. Death never is. But in my case, confusion was rampant. No one knew what to do. Really.

I was blessed with a few happy accidents that made my life much easier in that difficult time. In the hours or days following Trudy's death, I had insisted that I be listed

as spouse on the death certificate. At the time, it was an emotional priority for me and an outrage to be described as anything less. I became almost rabidly fixated on the issue. And at that specific point in history, it was unclear to everyone what my actual status was. Mercifully, and with the stroke of a pen, the county coroner's office noted me as such.

I was a widow. It was a sleight of hand that made my life easier to bear in the transactions that followed. Though for all intents and purposes it was, perhaps arguably, not true. Recall—we were not recognized as married in Michigan, the state that we called home and the state where Trudy died.

continued...

But that status became like a badge of honor to me. One I certainly never wanted, but nonetheless, I wore it like a crown. On more than one occasion I know that I benefited from someone on the other side of the counter making the decision not to challenge the term. A sympathetic look and knowing nod, so many small kindnesses and courtesies shown to me that I am so grateful for.

And then, in June 2015, the Supreme Court took the action that Trudy and I had only dreamed of, validating our marriage across the nation. She wasn't here to celebrate with me but I celebrated. And I certainly cried.

It is astonishing the amount of stress or weight that is lifted from you at such a moment in time. I can only liken it to having dropped a heavy coat that you were not even aware that you had on; walking a little taller in your own shoes, head up, eyes on the horizon—feeling like you counted, daring the world, almost, to call you anything less than their equal. And breathing, deeply . . . almost as if for the first time.

I have walked in those shoes every day since that ruling. I have taken those deep breaths, dropping behind me holdover remnants of

the heavy burden carried for too long. It is validating. Invigorating. It is peaceful.

And so now, this.

On this day—my third wedding anniversary. This.

This campaign, this election, and these seemingly endless tirades of hatred and divisiveness. All of this has brought into sharpened focus for me, the journey of my past three years—of a lifetime, really.

The cup of equality is a good cup. Once tasted, it is hard to resist.

It is what is at stake here.

Of course, I have no concrete proof yet of this new president's actions versus his intentions—of what he says he'll do versus what he will (actually) do.

I have only fear. And exhaustion. And anger.

Fear of what may happen. And let's be honest, anyone paying attention to the people being put into positions of power fears what may happen.

And I'm tired. So tired.

And after a fashion, a version of my story is

I am angry that in so doing, a very large portion of America is holding up that heavy coat for me (and people like me) to slip back into again.

why we, the people of my community, are all so tired. We have fought for everything—even when we didn't know that we were fighting—we were fighting. For each simple step, in countless ways throughout our lives. We had only just begun to believe, to breathe, and now this.

It is unconscionable. And of course, it is why I am so angry.

Let me be clear. I am not angry that people I know (and don't know) voted for a candidate that I did not support. I am not angry that a party I did not support won the election.

I am angry that in so doing, a very large portion of America is holding up that heavy coat for me (and people like me) to slip back into again.

And I just will not do it. I will not.

I will fight again. We all will.

For every single step.

And fair warning, I have a pretty fierce guardian angel on my shoulder for this fight. And any of you who knew Trudy know that that is true.

KAREN, MICHIGAN

My dad is a ninety-five-year-old climate change scientist, WWII vet, and Hillary supporter. He's been devastated by the election results. Inconsolable. He's a man who doesn't lose hope easily, and this new national climate of hatred and bigotry has made him feel dirty. Then, yesterday, he said, "If they have to have their wall, how about if we put solar panels on top, and wind turbines, and create sustainable communities all along it." Forever a visionary.

He gives me *radical hope.*

MAGDALENE, NEW YORK

It seems silly to call myself a "lifelong Republican" when I'm only thirty-one,

but the fact remains true. I've been the lone red dot in a very blue family for my entire life. I volunteered on W's reelection campaign and was a very vocal McCain supporter in 2008. I cried when Obama won. But as I've gotten more politically aware, I've realized the GOP isn't on the ground it claims it is. As I've gotten more socially aware, I've begun to struggle with my identity as a Republican—something I was always proud to say before I was whispering apologetically. When the party officially nominated Donald Trump, I printed out a new voter registration to register as an Independent—no way I could take the plunge all the way over to the Democrat side, to one I'd so long worked against.

I had a little bit of an identity crisis. I was never a party-line voter, but I still felt like I was redefining the very basis of who I was. Many of my Republican friends were also disillusioned this election cycle, but I found myself at odds with a lot of people I'd worked with and valued since I was a freshman in college. Suddenly, I was their enemy.

A friend added me to this group and I almost left at first. Sure, I was going to vote for Hillary, but I didn't feel like I belonged. I knew I wasn't the only Republican here, but I still felt like I was crashing someone else's party (literally). But I was *so* welcomed and *so* supported. I felt like I belonged. Even when discussing some of my views that are still rather conservative, I was respected. I've been in a GOP split-party haze for so long I forgot what it was like for my opinions to matter.

My license expired on Saturday, so on Thursday I went to the tax collector's office to prove who I was and get everything squared away. They asked if I needed to update my voter registration. I thought about the state of the GOP. I thought about my experiences posting and reading in this group. I thought about whether or not I should make such a big change. Did I *need* to update my voter registration? You know what . . . yeah, I did.

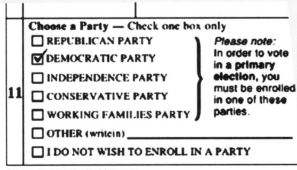

LAUREL ANN, FLORIDA

I have no profound words to say but thankfully, I don't need to—this awesome kid, my son Owen, has said it all with this innocent little drawing he made all on his own. It says, "Love is for everyone." We are with you. We are grateful for you. And we love you with no walls or boundaries.

ALEX H., ILLINOIS

I, an immigrant black woman, was sitting in my Toyota, eating Afghan food, listening to (blasting) reggae music. I noticed a Muslim man praying. I didn't think twice, I turned down my music out of respect. It's just a simple thing but it made me smile. I live in a world where this is okay. **Being decent costs nothing.**

ALICIA

Wishing everyone in this group all of our love from our silly crew in Illinois! These are our Trump-got-elected faces. *Say what?* This group gives me such hope and reading these stories is a welcome occurrence each day. If you ever see us in passing or with our stickers on the car, please reach out. We're in this together! Keep pushing and we will get through this. Much love, Pantsuit Nation.

MONET, ILLINOIS

My beautiful daughters.

My husband and I had the crazy idea to adopt children (at the ages of seventy-one and fifty-nine, respectively) and we love these girls to bits. We live in the "blue bubble" of Portland, Oregon, and I will keep our girls away from discrimination based on their race and gender as long as I can, even choosing to change our vacation plans to stay out of the red states. I made the mistake of complacency during the election, believing that no one could possibly vote for Donald Trump, and that he was just a reality show star and silly man looking for attention. He wasn't even well spoken or charismatic. And women's rights, we won that battle a long time ago, right? How could I have been so wrong?

My girls have only lived during the Obama administration where the president's daughters have curly hair and skin like theirs. They attend a school which is diverse and inclusive. I say this because I believe I was lulled into a false sense of security because of my great good fortune to live in a liberal, progressive community and I thought my protest days were long behind me (think Vietnam peace march). "Leave it to the millennials," I said. I'm sorry. I'm sorry I wasn't making calls for Hillary to Ohio and Pennsylvania and Florida. I'm

sorry I didn't want to make waves with my male family members who voted for Trump but say they love me and love my girls. I'm sorry I didn't take Donald Trump seriously. I'm sorry I didn't see the danger until too late.

I won't make the same mistake again. Every chance I get to speak up, I will. Every petition, I'll sign. Every march, I'll be there with my girls. They know about love and compassion, teamwork and sharing. They need to know it doesn't exist for everyone and that they must be strong and proud and committed to "liberty and justice for all," not just those folks who can buy it.

I won't make the same mistake again. Every chance I get to speak up, I will. Every petition, I'll sign. Every march, I'll be there with my girls.

PENNY, OREGON

I have seen many posts saying, "We are all women," "I don't see color," or "What does race have to do with anything?"

This is not only dismissive, it's color-blind and very hurtful. I am a black, multiracial woman. My blackness shapes who I am as a woman; to deny me the recognition of my blackness is to deny a core part of me and my experience as a woman in this world.

There has been a lot of discussion about white privilege, intersectionality, racism, and microaggressions and how they all play a role in feminism. So I wrote this post. I realize it will make people uncomfortable or maybe even angry but I hope you sit with that discomfort and you hear me out so we can be a better and more inclusive space.

Privilege

These are the unearned and often hidden benefits given to you by society. It's not a dirty word, it's often used to show you that you need to stop and listen. Many people assume that privileged = rich, but there are many different types of privilege. These include but are not limited to the following: white, cisgender, heterosexual, able-body, hearing, Christian, male, etc. You can be privileged in one area, and lack privilege in another. I am a cis, able-bodied, heterosexual, black Christian woman. My privileges are (and not limited to): Christian, cis, heterosexual, able-bodied, hearing. I lack male and white privilege. It's important to learn what your privileges are because those are what society defaults to. Once you learn what privileges you have, you can start to learn how to push back on your privilege and use your privilege for those who don't have it.

Racism

You can't fully understand racism if you don't understand white privilege in our society. Racism by definition is power/privilege + racial prejudice. What is this power portion? This power comes from society . . . this is what society defaults to, which is white privilege. This is why reverse racism does not exist. People of color do not have the privilege or power element in society. Everyone can have racial prejudices. No one is immune to that. Just because your sister/brother/aunt/child/friend/partner is a person of color does not absolve you or exempt you from having racial bias or from doing/saying something racist. So when someone says XYZ is racist, don't say, "But I have this person of color so I can't be racist." Yes, you still can be.

Color-blindness

The above brings us to color-blindness. Many of us were taught not to see color and to be color-blind. We have to work to undo that. Color-blindness is a form of racism. This is because it ignores the real experiences that people of color have because they are people of color. It's absolutely fine to recognize that we are all different and unique. These differences make us who we are. Don't be afraid of them; embrace them. See me for me. See me as a black woman, not just a woman. Recognize that these identities are what shape me.

continued...

Microaggressions

These are what I call accidentally racist statements. Things like "You speak well for a black girl," or "Where are you from? No, really, where are you from?" These are harmful because they *other* the person and also serve to reinforce harmful stereotypes.

Intersectional Feminism

This is important. Feminism has a long history of only working toward the advancement of white women and leaving women of color behind. We need intersectional feminism to advance all women. We need to know that while we are working toward equality, we have to remember and work to advance the issues that plague our trans sisters and our sisters of color. Each of these communities has unique and different issues, and we have to work toward them too.

We need to know that while we are working toward equality, we have to remember and work to advance the issues that plague our trans sisters and our sisters of color.

So now what?

1) Do not ignore our voices.

2) Don't minimize our struggles.

3) Learn when to stop talking and listen and when to use your voice to educate.

4) Stop telling us color doesn't matter. It does and saying it doesn't is racist.

5) Keep yourself educated on the issues, follow BIPOC, LGBTQIA, and other marginalized groups' pages.

6) Get comfortable being uncomfortable when people say, "Hey, that's offensive/hurtful/racist." Apologize. Don't double down, don't say, "I'm sorry, but . . ." or "I'm sorry; that's not my intention." Just, "I'm sorry."

7) Keep other white people (and other privileged people) in check. Call in your fellow privileged people.

8) Ask what the marginalized communities need and listen to the members for answers.

9) We don't want your sympathy; we want your solidarity.

10) Don't center the conversation around yourself if we are telling you our truth. It is not the same nor is it helpful.

I wanted to write this so that we as Pantsuit Nation can come together and make sure we work and continue to work as an inclusive group where we all feel accepted and loved. This means learning hard stuff and being uncomfortable and not being afraid to be uncomfortable. Uncomfortable is good; that is how we grow.

> *Uncomfortable is good; that is how we grow.*

GRACE, WASHINGTON

I am an Indian-American woman from a Muslim immigrant family

and one-half of a married interracial lesbian couple. I have spent my entire life trying to break the stereotypes that are associated with every facet of my identity, and I'm proud to say that I have managed to stay positive and annoyingly optimistic through it all. Last week, though, with the results of the election, some of my unerring optimism shifted to fear and resentment. How could this country that was coming to accept who I am have allowed someone who stands for everything I'm not to be elected? It is still shocking and unreal even almost one week later.

That said, I have taken this time to regain my optimism. To see beyond the nasty actions of what I believe to be a minority of Trump supporters. To believe that the United States is still a beautiful country full of opportunity, openness, and love. To hope that I am still a valued member of my community and of this society. You see, I have to believe all this in order to continue to be *who I am.* I know that everyone in this group has feelings similar to mine and I have written this post in the hopes that I can spread a little of my optimism on to you. Also, here's a picture of my wife and me on our wedding day. This is the kind of love that exists in this country. Please don't forget.

I am a proud Arab American.

I just finished this batch of baklava, which will go on my Thanksgiving table as it does every year, right between the pumpkin pie and the pecan pie. In 2010, I entered my baklava in the Minnesota State Fair and won a red ribbon (second place). Whenever I hear about someone bad-mouthing Arabs, Muslims, or any other group for that matter, I just want to sit them down with some baklava for a nice chat. It seems impossible that we wouldn't be able to find common ground over something so delicious. Perhaps we would only argue about where baklava comes from. Baklava: The Great Peace Negotiator. Well, unless you are allergic to nuts or gluten . . . in which case I could offer you a damn good hummus, and we could still argue about its country of origin. Please keep sharing your inspiring stories and words of encouragement. I know they are helping me. May you all find some common ground over delicious food in the next days, and Happy Thanksgiving!

DEENA, WASHINGTON

This holiday

my husband and I will be traveling to a red state from the liberal bastion of the New York / Connecticut area. As you can see we are proudly an interracial couple. I just wanted to share with this group, even though I walk with a constant fear of hate, especially wanting to protect my husband from those who want to attack us for our relationship, I also have found in this group a resolve to face that fear with a confidence that love trumps hate and that we need to stand proud and remind all of America that our family is as American as apple pie as well.

TIFFANY & TROY, CONNECTICUT

Happy Thanksgiving to you all from our American Muslim family.

This holiday has special meaning to us each year. Our parents arrived here as refugees fleeing a Ugandan dictator in November of 1972. A local church sponsored us and welcomed us with open arms, granting us the opportunity to start anew! Our parents worked hard to give us a good life and now we are working hard to give our children an even better life. With uncertainty ahead, we can only hope and pray for the best. This amazing nation has not let us down . . . we have faith that this continues. May God bless America—and may God bless us all!

SAFANA, VIRGINIA

I'm a Latina atheist

(or agnostic depending on the day) pictured here with my strong,
feminist fourteen-year-old daughter and beautiful devout Muslim
Nigerian and American "family" as we gathered on Thanksgiving
to rejoice in the love we have for one another, gratitude for our
complicated lives, and the unity we feel against the new political
reality. These are fierce and funny women who will not and cannot
be deterred by hate and who radiate love to all. I'm grateful for
people who I know will stand up for them and all of us.

AIXA, FLORIDA

The day after the election

I received a letter in my mailbox without a return address. It proceeded to explain that a "neighbor" had walked through my neighborhood and upon seeing my rainbow flag felt "uncomfortable." The letter went on to explain that my rainbow flag was disrespectful to the American flag. It was signed "your neighbor." Needless to say, I was shocked. I live in a very blue city in an even bluer neighborhood (unfortunately in a newly red state). A college town with a diverse population and my neighborhood reflects the diversity. Shaking and crying, I shared the letter immediately with a few neighbors. I also sent out a response to our neighborhood e-mail list. Please know I didn't think for a moment it was one of the people on my street. I believed it was someone close by who now felt emboldened to shame someone flying a flag in solidarity with LGBTQIA sisters and brothers. I had started flying the flag the day after the Pulse Orlando massacre. How did my wonderful, loving neighbors respond? They built a wall of flags. Love will always trump hate.

SUSAN, MICHIGAN

Just a couple of Muslim refugees (Iraqi civilians who worked as interpreters) and I together in Baghdad and now here in the US. I'm so thankful **I never let fear win** and got to know two of the greatest and selfless individuals I will ever know: men I consider to be my best friends and who sacrificed more for this country than 99.9 percent of those spewing nonsense and hate related to Muslims and refugees.

PETER, MASSACHUSETTS

I am an Armenian refugee

from Azerbaijan and I'm with her. I came to the US at fourteen years old after escaping ethnic cleansing in the former USSR. It took us two-plus years to receive refugee status while living in horrid conditions. In the last few years I've been asked often when do I intend to pay back the US for bringing me here. I always answer calmly, with facts, but the hurt doesn't easily go away.

I'm American, end of story, but not to them.

The pain these questions drenched in hatred cause cannot be passed on to my American-born children so I choose to show by actions. I often answer, "My parents paid back for the tickets to bring us to this country within two years. They started working five to six months after arriving after learning English and when the food stamps program for refugees ran out. I started working soon after turning fifteen. I paid for my own education in college and law school. We paid taxes since year one, before becoming citizens five years after arriving. We are investors, property owners, taxpayers with thriving careers in law, banking, and real estate. We volunteer, donate, and teach our children to love this country and to give back. And we are also public servants. This past year I ran and won my city's city council race by 64 percent of the vote. Most importantly we are American citizens and we love this country. I think we paid it back tenfold and we won't stop because what we have here—safety, freedom, opportunity—cannot be found anywhere else in this world and every refugee and immigrant knows this."

ANNA ASTVATSATURIAN TURCOTTE, MAINE

Immigrants.
Refugees.
Displaced people.

Foreigners. Regardless of the definitional categorization, I will continue to affirm that as a nation that believes in "life, liberty, and the pursuit of happiness," we must continue to safely and smartly be a welcoming nation to all. I don't care what the president-elect has to say about it. That's that, people. Today was another awesome day tutoring and bonding with the Rwandan family of refugees I mentor through Refugee Services of Texas.

(I totally get the whole "Are you smarter than a 5th grader thing" now, by the way. Helping them with their math and science homework momentarily had me questioning what I'm doing with this Ph.D.!)

NAOMI WHEELESS, TEXAS

The hardest part of the election for many of us is the outright acceptance of sexual assault. For me, it wasn't my rapist who caused me the most grief and pain. While the physical pain he inflicted on me was unforgivable, the true emotional toll was the silence of those around me.

This election is eerily similar to the rhetoric that was spewed at me when I reported my assault to police and campus authorities. I don't go a day without thinking how normalized rape has become in our culture and I can't help but fear for the future.

This photo is a part of a gender-based violence (GBV) campaign at my university, showcasing survivors and breaking the stigma of being a victim.

"In the end, we will remember not the words of our enemies, but the silence of our friends."

—DR. MARTIN LUTHER KING JR.

SARAH, MINNESOTA

Like many LGBTQIA couples here, my beloved and I were terrified at the meaning of a Trump-Pence administration. That night, we made the decision to, after over twelve years, make honest men of each other. Wednesday night, in a service officiated by my father, it became reality.

ADAM, NEW YORK

As someone with a physical disability,

I've spent my life sometimes feeling overlooked, excluded, and underestimated—doing everything I can think of to change the way society views the disabled community. My mantra has always been "I'm a person," and that's never been more true than right now. Thank you, Pantsuit Nation, for making me feel like a person—for affirming that, yes, I am a person! I matter! People with disabilities matter! I will never stop fighting for our rights and against bullies . . . I will never not be a person!

MELISSA, ILLINOIS

Last night my wife, Nikki,

and I went to see *Loving*, the story of Richard and Mildred Loving. A picture of them hangs on the wall of our dining room alongside old family photos, because while we are not related to them by blood we do feel a certain kinship with them, that they are ancestors of ours. They paved the way in America for families like ours, and we owe them a huge debt of gratitude. So it was compelling to watch their story being told on the silver screen, and I was brought to tears seeing these two reluctant heroes memorialized in this fashion.

At a time when some of my dearest friends fear their marriages will be invalidated because of campaign promises, I am thankful that my marriage, once considered by some to be radical and unholy, is safely protected by law. I was reminded what a privilege that is.

Thanks to Angela L. Owens, we made our own homage to the Lovings, re-creating their picture on our wall. I hope it serves as a constant reminder to my daughters that love trumps hate.

JEFF, NEW YORK

This is my son,

Mitchell. I adopted him when he was four days old. He was in my arms when he was thirty hours old. He was the love of my life in so many, many ways. He made me a mother. One of my favorite things to do was to sit at the dinner table for hours and talk to him about current events. About how to be kind, about how to use his social capital to help those who were not as favored, popular, and well-treated in his world. We talked often of immigration, racial issues, laws, fairness, justice, and love. When Obama was elected, I bought him a wonderful poster that included Rosa Parks, MLK Jr., and Obama all on the same page. It is still on the wall in his room.

When my son was almost fourteen, Trayvon Martin was murdered. My son took that hard. He internalized that deeply. He posted a picture on Facebook of himself in a hoodie and that he was "ready to die."

We will, as a people, survive this, but those who lose hope will not remain with us.

My son suffered from severe depression and anxiety his whole life. He was the most anxious toddler I had ever seen. His therapist helped us find ways to help him with this from as young as three-and-a-half.

When my sweet, handsome, smart, funny, and amazing son was sixteen, he lost that battle with depression and anxiety and he died by suicide. I have been numb with grief for two years since that day. This election has furthered my feelings of numbness. I am so shocked and saddened that so many people are now immediately more fearful, unsafe, and broken. I believe that there are many people who are struggling with feelings of hopelessness and anxiety which have now been exacerbated by this election, and who will likely have less access to care as we see assistance chipped away through the policies that will eat away at the help they need. We will lose people in our nation to suicide whose feelings of hopelessness have increased because of the awful and divisive climate empowered by the election of this man and the empowerment of his cabinet and staff. We will, as a people, survive this, but those who lose hope will not remain with us. I am so sad about this. Today, 117 people will die by suicide. If you are reading this, and you are thinking about harming yourself, please know that you matter. We need you. We will get through this and we are a powerful force. Stay.

MELISSA, ARIZONA

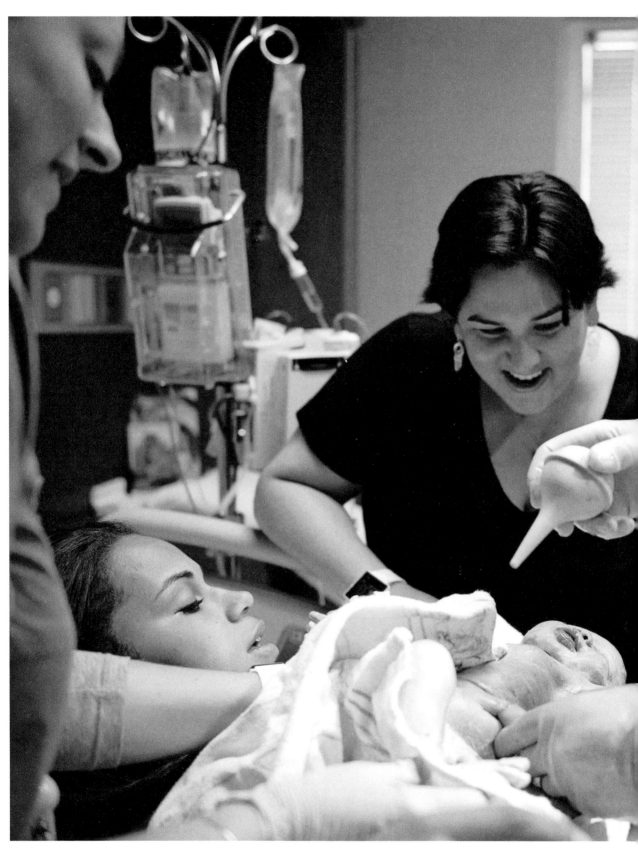

This is my family.

I was married at eighteen, a mother by twenty, and divorced by twenty-two. Years later I was pregnant once again, but this time I wasn't excited, or even happy—I was terrified. I did not want to raise another child. I wasn't in a relationship, I wasn't even sure which of the two men I had been seeing was the father. I considered every avenue, made phone calls we never expect to make and appointments at clinics that I previously thought were for trashy people. I thought I was trash. It's not until you are in another's shoes that you often see how misguided you are, how blind to others suffering you are. And how easily you can end up there, despite the precautions taken.

continued...

I do not believe we have a choice in who we are attracted to and who we love, but I did have a choice in who would raise this amazing boy.

And then I connected with these two amazing women, and felt in my bones that they were meant to be parents to my son. They changed me, whether they know it or not, into a much more open-minded and loving individual. My son changed me as well.

I am pro-choice, more so after becoming a birth mother than ever, because I have felt the pain and emotional roller coaster, health complications, etc. that women go through when they carry a child they do not parent. Abortion wasn't my choice, but I wouldn't ever push anyone to carry a child if they aren't mentally and emotionally prepared for it (and most women considering either option lack real support, something vital to climbing out of the darkness that's left postpartum).

I do not believe we have a choice in who we are attracted to and who we love, but I did have a choice in who would raise this amazing boy and I *chose* two women. Not because they were two women but because they laugh more than any two people I have ever met, are strong, smart, and full of love.

I was eight months' pregnant when I opened my newsfeed one morning and saw the Supreme Court ruling in favor of same-sex marriage equality. I bawled and called the people I wanted to talk to most, and we discussed whether there was time for a wedding before the birth or if they should wait until little man could be a part of the celebration. They waited, and six months later we partied down at a beautiful ceremony.

Please don't abandon those with different political viewpoints than yours.

I will fight every day for my family, blood and chosen. I will march in protest, and I will fight with information. I was born into an incredibly conservative Catholic family in Texas, had only ever voted for a Republican until this election, and previously rolled my eyes at friends who got excited for Pride because to me it just meant lots of traffic. Please don't abandon those with different political viewpoints than yours. Had my friends, who continued to spread information and knowledge and slowly won me to their side, given up on me, and walked away, I wouldn't have been in a place to find these women, people with whom my soul will always share a connection.

I am a birth mother, a single mother, I am a minority, and I am so happy to be a part of Pantsuit Nation where love trumps hate.

RACHEL, TEXAS

Fifteen years ago,

I was promoted to sergeant while on deployment. After leaving the Marine Corps, I sometimes wondered where most of my military friends went. Years later Facebook was invented, and it was nice catching up. It was great chatting with some old friends and life was good.

I never had the courage to post anything personal on my Facebook account. I had only come out to my immediate family and my mother urged me to not be so vocal about my sexuality.

2015 came around and by this time I had been with my husband for eight years. We were expecting a daughter, and our marriage would be recognized in the US. I made several posts. I announced the birth of our daughter. I announced I was married to a man, and I didn't care.

I swore an oath in the summer of 1999 that I would protect my country against all enemies, foreign or domestic, and **Trump will never be my president.**

Today I have five friends left out of the forty-some military buddies who had added me years ago. Some unfriended me after finding out I was gay. Others left when they found out I was legally married, but the majority left when I posted that I stood with her.

I never thought I would feel this way again. Growing up "different" in a very conservative town was enough for me to want to leave. And now that feeling resurfaced.

But we Marines are tough. We endured one of the toughest boot camps the world had to offer. We survived thirteen weeks of hell. We survived deployments and we are resilient by nature. We will survive that orange turd.

I swore an oath in the summer of 1999 that I would protect my country against all enemies, foreign or domestic, and Trump will never be my president.

I stand with her.

I'm a feminist. I'm a father. I'm the son to a single Mexican mother (who is now a US citizen) who came to the US in hopes of giving me a better future. I'm me. And I love this group.

It is people like you that have made it possible for people like my family to be able to succeed in this country. Thank you all for being you. Thank you for being open-minded and for welcoming everyone with open arms.

ADRIAN De LUNA, TEXAS

This happened to me several months ago.

I was exiting a hair salon when I accidentally bumped a woman or she purposely bumped me. I said, "Oh, I am sorry." There were two women and they loudly said, "Muslim, go back to Syria." In my head, I thought, "Would it help if I said I am Mexican American and Catholic? No, I am sure it wouldn't. But even if I was Muslim, so what?" I remember my mom always saying we were part Native American. So I told the two women my ancestors probably welcomed their pilgrim ancestors' boat.

Then I went to my car and cried.

SYLVIA, CALIFORNIA

I really want to share a little bit about my grandmother.

My nana is a Muslim refugee who does not speak English, and who now lives in a nursing home on the government's dime—in other words, she may be the epitome of what a certain population of our country hates right now. My nana has lived with me since I was born, and immigrated to the US with my parents and me in the early 1990s, escaping the war in Bosnia—the worst tragedy to occur in Europe since WWII. She raised me while my parents learned English, worked, and assimilated into American life. I have always called my nana my third parent.

This election season has brought to the surface a lot of hate against people like my nana and the rest of my family. There are so many false narratives out there, misconceptions, and very dangerous rhetoric. Regardless of the election's outcome, this country has become a little bit

continued...

scarier to me. The people who believe the vile things about us are not going to magically disappear, even under a non-Trump presidency. My parents constantly draw comparisons between the rhetoric we see here in the US and the rhetoric they saw in Yugoslavia shortly before all the havoc. I don't think people realize how easily those kinds of events can repeat themselves if society doesn't put a stop to the catalysts.

When my nana escaped from Bosnia, she had to do so secretly. She spent almost two days stuck on a bus going toward Turkey, praying that it wouldn't get stopped. But she's been here for me from the day I was born, taking care of me, babysitting my friends as well, taking me on walks to feed the birds and donate old clothes, cooking for us, teaching me my dos and don'ts, giving me a beautiful childhood that I look back on in awe. When we first got to the US, we lived in dangerous neighborhoods ridden with poverty and violence. I have no memories of this. My family protected me fiercely, and I never ever felt like I was missing anything.

Almost two years ago, my nana had

I don't think people realize how easily those kinds of events can repeat themselves if society doesn't put a stop to the catalysts.

a stroke. She is no longer able to live with our family, for she needs nurses by her side 24/7, just in case. It has taken a deep toll on my heart to watch her deteriorate, and not have her warm spirit in our family home. Without her, I would most definitely not be the woman I am today, and the woman I continue becoming.

It has hurt my heart deeply to think that people like this can be seen as scary or worthless members of our country. I have my whole life to defend and prove myself, but my nana has already done her part. Why is that not enough? I feel like this country has a certain group of people who would squash us like bugs if someone needed to get thrown under the bus. Donald Trump puts this kind of vile and ignorant rhetoric on a platform, making those people feel validated in their dangerous beliefs. I wish the world was above this. I wish everyone could see the danger of what this man stands for. I wish they'd educate themselves about the people they think they should fear.

My nana is my hero. I am privileged and blessed, definitely—but also scared. I am deeply confident in what I believe is right, and I will fight for that for my whole life. But I think acceptance is not a partisan issue. Trump does not represent a specific political mind-set; he ultimately represents ignorance, scapegoating, and danger. I wish people could see that they do not have to be a part of that.

She's four. She's Hispanic and Caucasian.

She's a girl growing up with a president who will ruin much of the progress made in the past eight years. With that as my fuel, she will learn and know what it is to be a strong woman. I'm embarrassed to say that was not a priority for me and my husband until this election. When Trump started saying awful things about Mexicans, I started getting uncomfortable. When Trump picked his gay-hating VP running mate, I started getting worried. When the Trump tape came out clearly saying in his own words that he regularly sexually assaults women, I started getting pissed. When people started saying it was locker room talk, I made a promise that my baby girl would know that her body is her own, that no one is allowed to touch her wherever or whenever they want unless she says they can, that when a man talks to her chest instead of her face, they will be the brunt of embarrassment and be sorry for doing that.

I feel like I've wasted the last four years making sure she knew she was pretty and was our little princess. Now she will know she is also smart, strong, that she has a voice and that voice matters.

JESSICA, ARIZONA

I am a mixed-race

(Scottish, English, Irish, Native American, and what was listed on my great-grandmother's census record as "black")

woman.

I am a college-educated, thirty-year-old, single mom. I work in the computer technology field.

My father was a Vietnam veteran, drafted into service, who suffered with depression and alcoholism after the war. He eventually died when I was fifteen from lung cancer caused by Agent Orange. It was both the most devastating and lucky turn in my life. You see, the VA paid for a portion of my college costs. He made me promise to make something of myself.

So I did. He gave me a locket while he was dying and I didn't put his photo in it until I graduated from college, despite working two jobs, maintaining a household, and raising a child alone, while I went to school full-time. I had food stamps for a while too.

Just because I had it hard doesn't mean that those rising behind me should suffer too. I want to make things easier for the next generation of women like me.

We are tough. We are powerful. We are the future.

In my county, 89 percent of voters voted for Trump. I felt alone. I felt like no one understood. I was afraid. I've not seen any blatant acts of hate, but I know that 89 percent of the people around me are silently hateful. It breaks my heart.

Then I found you. All of you. I found your hope, your love, your support, your enormous range of difference and your sameness. I found faith in the beauty of a fifteen-year-old boy in his Hillary tee, a beautiful neighborhood of rainbow flags, a family of skin tones from night to day, each one radiant and more so together. I found a nurse helping someone after a car accident. I found a Syrian neighbor at your door. I found a couple in their perfect wedding dresses, and a family beautiful because they weren't "traditional." I found a man in Texas, with a hat and a beard, and a welcome sign. I found a woman raising her voice for another on a bus.

I know that with each of us here, we'll be okay.

I love you all, maybe selfishly. I love you for reminding me that my home is beautiful. I'm proud again to be American because each of you gave me strength when I was broken. Thank you.

LEANNA, GEORGIA

We are
tough.
We are
powerful.
We are
the future.

Sending love from our Persian, Latino, black, gay, straight, liberal Hillary-loving *modern* family.

ROXANA AMINI & DAVID DURÁN, CALIFORNIA

Give your thoughts a trim, my friend.

A couple of weeks ago, I was getting a haircut in a Twin Cities hair salon. The staff was nice enough to accommodate my special need for a private place and a no-man zone while my hijab was off. The salon has a higher, more private platform level where I can have my hair cut.

It was slightly busier than usual. I sat down and removed my head covering, placing it in my bag, then chatted away with my hairdresser. As we started working on a hairstyle, another hairdresser came back from the washing area with her client and settled in their station across from us. Neither of them had seen me coming in wearing my hijab before starting their conversation.

As I was flipping through a magazine and sipping my coffee, I heard the words, "Sharia law." I saw another hairdresser looking at me as if she was aware of something I was not. I then overheard more of their conversation.

Hairdresser: " . . . them and the Sharia law they practice . . ."

Client: "Yeah. . . . Did you know they are implementing the Sharia law in our public schools?"

Then they continued discussing the practice of polygamy whereby a man can have "eight wives."

"It's actually three," the other corrected.

I sank in my seat and listened. I reached out to my phone and texted my husband for advice. He replied back: "Do what you do best—after your haircut though." So I did.

As I walked toward the checkout, I asked my hairdresser to call her colleague over so I could talk to her. She went to the other station and asked the hairdresser, then came back saying, "I am sorry she cannot come and speak to you. She is with her client." I then asked my hairdresser to go back and ask her if I could come to her station and talk to her for few minutes. She did and came back with the same message. The other hairdresser was "unavailable."

By then the assistant manager had noticed my attempts to engage in a conversation and asked if I wanted to leave a message for the hairdresser. Seeing no other option, I accepted. She gave me a piece of paper and this is what I wrote:

"Dear Friend, I overheard the conversation with your client talking about Sharia law

continued...

and Islamic practices. As a Muslim woman, I want to ask if you have a Muslim friend or an Islamic source where you get your information. I believe we need to be more informed in our conversations, making them part of the solution and not part of the problem. I would like to be your new Muslim friend. I really hope you'll reach out to me to meet for a coffee or chat whenever you are free."

I then left my name and phone number in the hopes that she would actually call. I am still waiting.

A few days ago I was working out with my friend at the gym, which is located in the same building as the hairdresser complex. The assistant manager came up to me with a shaky voice and trembling hands, thanking me for my letter and gracious approach.

"Your letter brought a lot of people to tears and I want to apologize for what you had to go through in our salon." I took her words as permission to give her a sweaty hug. Then we had an awesome conversation about unity, diversity, and Lebanese food.

"Forgive my comment, but we are not really used to having people from your community come across with such grace," she said. I couldn't agree more.

"It's my Islamic teaching that compelled me to reach out, modeling my prophet Muhammad, peace be upon him, in his mercy and compassion," I replied. "Please tell that hairdresser I am still hoping she will call," I concluded.

I know there are a lot of people in Minnesota, and indeed throughout the US, having similar conversations. My hope is that we will have the courage to talk about these uncomfortable topics and reach out to one another with nothing but love.

> *I believe we need to be more informed in our conversations, making them part of the solution and not part of the problem.*

HANADI CHEHABEDDINE, MINNESOTA

At the age of seventy-seven,

my father came out as transgender and I couldn't be more proud. Regardless of your age, it is never too late to live your truth. I love you, Ann!

ELISA KUCHVALEK, FLORIDA

No one can
take away your
happiness...
Eight months married
to my best friend...
Love is Love
is love .

I'm a thirty-year-old woman and a lifelong Florida resident.

As someone who came from a Jewish family and has always resided in an area comprised of a large Jewish population, we learned "never again" from an early age. We knew of the Holocaust, had many classmates whose grandparents gave presentations to our classes about their experiences, and knew we had to be a voice against racism in all forms. Growing up, my mother was the loudest voice encouraging me to always stand up for women's rights and for everyone who was being discriminated against. As a child, she would tell me to never forget that hatred and racism is alive in people's hearts and we have to always stand up and fight it.

Despite considering myself a feminist and an activist from as early as I can remember, I realize now that my efforts haven't been enough. I have felt a nagging pain in my soul since the election, the kind of pain that makes me grateful my grandmother—my Bubbie— passed away before she had to see this all unfold again before her eyes.

I married my high school sweetheart when we were twenty-three, and at twenty-five we welcomed our first child into this world: our beautiful, sweet son. Coming from a small family, I knew I wanted a big family. I wanted

continued...

my son to have siblings and a loud, chaotic home filled with laughter and joy. I got pregnant with our second child when our son was two years old and learned we were having a little girl. We decided on the name Wylie and our son helped us paint a nursery for the sister he could not wait to meet. When I was 27.5 weeks pregnant, we learned that Wylie would not survive. She was diagnosed in utero with a series of rare, fatal heart defects that made her incompatible with life.

I wish I could describe the pain of hearing those words: *incompatible with life*. A part of me died with her diagnosis, feeling the daughter I loved and wanted move within my body and knowing that she would inevitably die. I, along with the support of my incredible husband, decided that I wanted to let Wylie go in peace and with dignity. However, the state of Florida felt that they knew my body better than I did. They thought they knew what was best for my baby more than I did. The state of Florida felt like I did not deserve the right to decide what to do for my baby, with my body, and I was sent home after a physician apologized that his hands were tied due to Florida's abortion laws. Forcing women— grieving mothers—to incubate death is unacceptable.

This is the moment when I realized that my body was not my own. It never was. Despite all of my years branding myself as an activist and a feminist, I learned it was never enough: I did not and do not own my body, nor does any woman.

There is little, if anything, worse in life than losing a child. What was once my life of joy and privilege became a black hole that swallowed me and my will to live. I pushed on because of my son, who was the only reason I had to go on. Each day, it became harder to go on. Each day, his smile was what ensured that I kept going on even when I didn't want to.

My son is now five. This past February, we adopted our beautiful, incredible, brilliant daughter at birth. To say she saved our lives is an understatement. She hung the sun back in my pitch-black sky the first moment I held her in my arms, filled with honor that someone chose me to be her mother. There will never be an honor greater.

When we brought our daughter home, I was unfriended on Facebook by the mother of a former playmate of my son's. She sent me a message to clarify that she was appalled we chose to adopt a child of color. She was frustrated, she said, by the fact I care "only about black lives." (We are very big supporters of the Black Lives Matter movement and I suppose this infuriated her, for some reason.) This was the first time that I, firsthand, experienced racism and bigotry out in the open in front of my face. I wish I could say it was the last time. We've had people shake their heads at us, giggle and insinuate that my husband was too stupid to notice his wife obviously had an affair, or ask, "What is she?" as they stare into my daughter's beautiful face. ("She's a baby," my son responds.)

My heart aches for the country that my children are forced to grow up in. When our son woke up and learned that Donald Trump had won, he had two questions: What is going to happen to our beloved family friends who had just married a couple of months earlier—were they going to be okay? And what would happen to his sister—was she going to be okay? At home, my children learn that love always wins. At home, our only religion is kindness and goodness and compassion. We believe that all human beings are equal, that no human being is illegal, and that our job is to always, *always* fight for equal rights for all people. My children are fortunate to have a feminist father who treats me, their mother, as an equal partner. They are fortunate to have many friends who live by the same moral compass that we do. But I also realize there is a world outside of our home and away from our safe little bubble. My children aren't in school yet, but my son soon will be. And I worry . . .

In my daughter Wylie's memory, I will never stop fighting for women's rights—which are human rights, after all. As a woman whose womb carried a terminal baby and as an adoptive mom, I have made it my duty to be at the forefront of the fight for women's rights. Abortion can be a painful choice, and, as so many brave Pantsuiters have shared, it can also be an easy choice. I believe in safe, legal, stigma-free abortion for all women making the choice, no questions asked.

I am often asked if being an adoptive mother changes my stance on reproductive rights. To be frank, it only fans the flames in my heart. As an adoptive mom, the "just adopt" explanation provided so coldly by Pence and other politicians is so callous. It dehumanizes birth mothers and the loss and pain they're forced to live with every day. It trivializes their heartbreak, their struggle, and it completely treats women as if they are wombs instead of people. I have always been completely pro-choice, but I am even more so after adoption touched my life.

We can't give up. We owe our children so much more than this.

> *In my daughter Wylie's memory, I will never stop fighting for women's rights—which are human rights, after all.*

LINDSAY, FLORIDA

This is my son and I,

and we are Muslim. Even though I was not born into that faith I knew after meeting so many people whose dignity, ethics and charity, kindness, and integrity was so inspiring that I had to join them too. My son has protected others at his school with such great bravery and strength it is awe inspiring, and yet a girl came up to him at his Montessori school (with plenty of DT supporting parents), to ask him if all Muslims were terrorists, and to inform him that because he wasn't Christian he would burn in hell. My son's response? Jesus is our prophet too, and we don't believe that this is who he was. He was better than that, and you know nothing about your own faith. Now, at his new school, a private Catholic school, he is well respected, and held in great esteem by the faculty and children too. His social studies teacher asked him to teach them about Islam. At the Catholic school, they love Yousef. Love comes to us in the most surprising places.

GINA & YOUSEF, PENNSYLVANIA

There I was standing on Election Night—thirty feet from where Hillary should have accepted the presidency.

Like a lot of you, the last month has been emotionally brutal. I'm terrified, I'm angry, and I've been asking myself what I can do to make this right.

Some of you may know me from Gamergate—a scandal that rocked the video game industry. Women in our field were targeted by violent gamers—threatened with rape, murder, and everything in between by men angry about the growing movement for inclusion.

The similarities between Gamergate and Trump's base are terrifying—both movements based in wanting to revert culture and establish white male supremacy.

Both are a backlash from the privileged who like things just as they are. The women targeted by Gamergate had our private lives violated, and when they couldn't find dirt, they just made things up. One of the worst parts for me was being targeted by Breitbart and Steve Bannon. The idea of him being the third-most-powerful person in the White House is terrifying to me.

During Gamergate, the men of our field chose to do nothing. Nothing changed until brave women stood up and fought back—often at extreme cost. Now that we're living in Gamergate America, I don't know what to do besides fight back again.

That's why I'm very strongly considering running for the legislature during 2018.

The only people that helped me during Gamergate were other women. Women journalists, women legislators, women prosecutors. I think it's more crucial than ever for women to have our voices represented in government—making laws and refusing to compromise when the marginalized bear the brunt.

It's my hope that I'm not the only woman thinking about running. Without our voices, the Democratic Party will never take the issues of women, black people, Muslims, LGBTQIA, Latinx, and other marginalized groups seriously. It's time for us to step up and commit ourselves to public service.

Hillary, you ran the marathon bravely. You broke barriers, and shattered the glass ceiling. It's time for us to take that baton and run the next leg of the race.

BRIANNA WU, MASSACHUSETTS

Hello, my name is Faggy Dyke.

Let me back up and explain. You see, today I got to experience my first "official" introduction to Trump's America. Also known as the next four years of my life.

As per my normal routine, I dropped off the kids and headed over to the neighborhood doughnut and coffee shop. As I was pulling into the parking lot, a car sped past me to get the spot I was headed to. No big deal. I gestured, "Go ahead, you're obviously in more hurry than I am." Again, no big deal. I had extra time.

As I walked in, the woman who cut me off was ahead of me in line. The cashier made small talk and asked her how her morning was. Her response took me by surprise. "It was going well, until that"—looking at me—"faggy dyke cut me off."

Now of course, 4,200 thoughts ran through my mind. Mostly resulting in her in a hospital and me in jail. Not a good plan. I was more shocked because normally people don't look at me and think "gay." I didn't feel any more gay this morning when I got dressed. So I'm not sure what gave her the idea. Either way, it was shocking.

While I was plotting her demise, a small voice reminded me, "When they go low, we go high." So I cut her off (intentionally in line) and said to the cashier, "Please ring me up for my usual and pay for her order as well."

I then turned to the lady and told her to enjoy her order on behalf of all the faggy dykes in the world and to have a sparkly day.

I *wish* I had a pocketful of glitter to toss in the air as I walked away.

Welcome to our new country, folks.

JIA HOWARD, ARIZONA

FUTURE
EMALE

At thirty-six, I find myself unemployed for the first time in twenty years.

I have always worked. Service jobs, child care, sales, clerical . . . In these fields and in life in general, I deal with misogynistic BS all the time. In the job that I had for the last thirteen years I worked my way from entry-level phone answering to managing half of the department in a very male-dominated field. I outlasted too many administrative changes to count, each time collecting more responsibilities because nobody else wanted them. Every step of the way I was training new employees that were hired at a higher pay than I was making.

My most recent supervisor exemplified everything wrong with people in that field. I figured I would continue working hard and outlast him. After six months of gradually being stripped of all but the most entry-level responsibilities and access, and being gaslighted throughout, I lost it.

I spoke out.

I corrected lies he told.

I contradicted him.

And I got fired.

I was suddenly an unemployed single mother. Do you have any idea how difficult it is to find a job that pays a living wage and covers before- and after-school child care costs?

I am not too proud to dig ditches, scrub toilets, or wait tables. I have before. I have great respect for people that do these necessary jobs and take pride in their work.

I would gladly take any shift, but there are no child care options after business hours. Definitely not any I could afford by working those hours.

After five months of fruitless job searching, I was resigned to move myself and my sons in with my parents and take the next entry-level position I found. Then I discovered that my local career center was sponsoring a six-week welding program at the local trade school. It's not extensive enough to include certification. But it's knowledge, and all knowledge is worth having. It's an introduction to a practical skill that will open opportunities. I demanded to be admitted.

I am working hard, and loving every second of it. My instructor proctors the hiring exam for one of the largest local employers. And I will ask for criticism and I will practice until I am ready to pass those exams.

I am not delusional, I know that I will continue to face misogyny at my future jobs.

But with my jacket on, nobody can stare at my chest.

With my pants on, nobody will tell me I should wear skirts and heels.

With my helmet down, nobody will tell me I should smile more or wear more makeup or style my hair.

And even if they did, I wouldn't be able to hear them over the beautiful buzzing sound of a perfect arc running a bead.

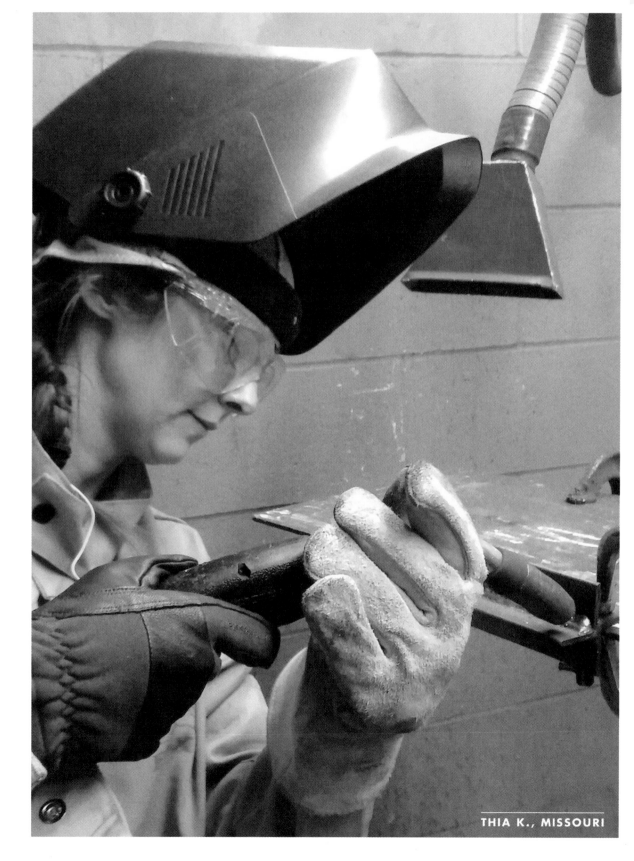

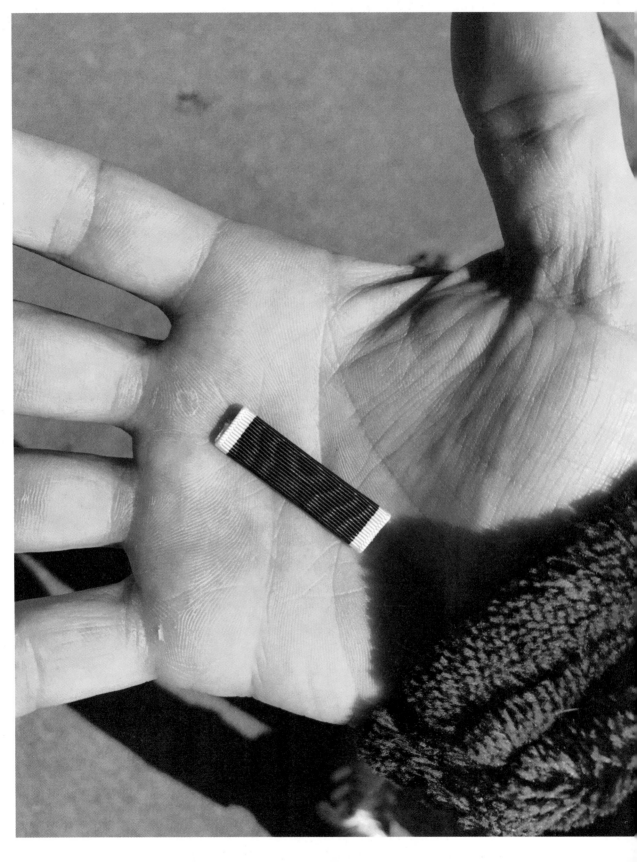

I don't know why I've kept this in my bag all these years.

This ribbon, which was awarded alongside the Purple Heart Medal, used to be in the top row of medals on my uniform. Now, I keep it with me instead because it's the only medal I've earned that I wish I could give back, but I can't. I suppose it's a reminder. On that fated day, I wish I could have seen the insurgent with an RPG sooner, and protected my soldiers better. I wish it would have detonated on the hill it ricocheted off of instead of detonating over my head. I wish my commanders had ignored it and not reported my injuries so I could have avoided recognition and remained just like everyone else who sacrificed mentally, but perhaps not physically during our time in combat.

But this medal also reminds me what I don't wish for: that anyone else would have been in my place that day to take the blast. Now, having hung up my uniform and Green Beret, it keeps reminding me that we all make sacrifices to protect those we love. I paid but a small price for freedom the day I earned this, and the years afterward spent in combat zones around the world. And it helps to remember that that price was small, and just one of many contributions we make on a daily basis to build a better world for future generations.

After this election, this medal has new meaning for me. It now embodies the memory of the trials and tribulations faced by members of our community as we push for equality and justice. It reminds me that we all take risks to believe in a better future, and suffer setbacks as we work for that future. For me it symbolizes the sacrifices we must make to continue championing the causes that have been recently washed out of mainstream thought by the cacophony of vitriol and the angst of a changing world. Lastly, I hope my voice inspires someone else to take that extra step or go that extra mile toward a more equal union for all. I'm a soldier and I fought and sacrificed for the things I believe in, because I believe in feminism, I believe in equal opportunity, and I believe in equal justice for all.

Here I am at my job, where I work with the public, in South Carolina, wearing a hijab. I am so relieved to have found this space where I can share my thoughts freely.

I can't have a "bad day" with customers. I feel like I have to be on my A-game always: super friendly, even with outright rude people. It isn't my nature anyway to be anything but polite and respectful (growing up in the South and raised by traditional Arab Muslim parents). But . . . I feel a responsibility to lay on the nice, friendly, cheerful extra because of my hijab. Because I feel like I'm perpetually a spokesperson for my faith. And I have to really know my stuff and speak with confidence. I feel looks of doubt when clients first see me.

On the bright side, though, my hope is that every person who comes in never having met or talked to a Muslim woman leaves thinking and telling their family and friends, "They aren't oppressed. They are smart, they are compassionate and helpful, and we should treat them with the same dignity I was treated with."

This responsibility feels like a burden at times, I won't lie. But if I can change even a handful of hearts and minds, invoke more humanity, and emphasize our commonality, it will all be worth it.

LAILA, SOUTH CAROLINA

I'm a bad hombre.

I am also a man who regularly uses the women's restroom.

At first glance you can see I am profoundly disabled as I move around in one of those bulky power wheelchairs. You can see braces holding my head and I'm skeleton-like thin. A computer screen hangs directly in front of my face. I cannot speak and I am a quadriplegic. Yet some consider me a threat to women and girls because I have a penis.

An insidious disease, ALS, has wreaked havoc on my body. When I leave my home I need two caregivers to guide my chair, carry all my equipment, and tend to my needs. So it is no easy task to move me around. The choice of which restroom to use is based on the sex of my caregivers. It is usually my wife, Judy, and daughter or my full-time nurse. If you thought after seeing all of this that anyone would see me as a threat you would be wrong.

Last summer we were out and I needed to use the restroom. As we were struggling my chair past a women's room door that didn't want to open wide, a teenage girl helped us by holding the door open. Once we were in, a middle-aged woman stated I should not be in there. Judy explained the situation and said we will be out of the way very soon when the woman exclaimed, "But he's a man!" My mind raced through several funny retorts, enough to make me laugh to myself. (This was one of those times when everyone who knows me all agree that it is good I could not speak.) Judy told the woman to step aside and then headed for the handicapped stall without any fanfare. Just taking care of business.

A little understanding and tolerance goes a long way in making my life better.

The last thing my caregivers need is more to deal with. A little understanding and tolerance goes a long way in making my life better.

My troubles using public restrooms pales in comparison to those who are transgender. At least people don't call me names or threaten me with bodily harm. I have little fear anyone is going to bully me.

Soon my state, Texas, will likely pass legislation to restrict trans women's and men's choices. We need to stop sexualizing the restroom and think of its true purpose.

STUART, TEXAS

My wife works for a local nonprofit organization

that hosts an annual holiday open house. A couple of days after the election, she texted me and asked if I'd be willing to be Santa for an hour or so at this event and take pictures with kids. I'm kind of an introvert so my first instinct is always to resist those kinds of things, but after I gave it some thought, I said yes. I felt like I needed to do something to put some good energy out in the world after the election and I know they were trying to find some diverse Santas.

Long story short, the suit was ill-fitting, they had no beard, the hat kept slipping down over my eyes (they *are* a nonprofit, after all, so we work with what we have). But the look of pure joy on the faces of some of the kids when they got to talk to a Santa who looked like them made it all worth it. I even overheard one girl telling her older brother, "I don't care if his beard isn't white. *That's Santa*." And she may not be my kid, but I was so proud that she asked Santa for a science kit.

So, from the frumpiest, unlikeliest Santa to ever hand out candy canes, Happy Holidays, Pantsuit Nation. No matter what you're celebrating this season, a little bit of good in the world can go a long way.

MICHAEL, NEBRASKA

Today I'm graduating with my master of science in educational human resource development from *the* Texas A&M University and am representing for all of us...in a pantsuit of course.

The cashier at Hobby Lobby asked if PSN were my initials. I said no...it's for Pantsuit Nation. She gave me a knowing look and said, "You go, girl!"

J. A., TEXAS

This is my four-year-old son, Emerson.

When he turned three, he didn't have any words. Not *Mama*. Not *Bye-bye*. Not *I love you*.

We were told he had speech delays. He started integrated preschool and we were told he had sensory-processing issues. We went to specialists. We spent hours and hours and a small fortune on therapy. He was diagnosed with autism. I felt relief because finally—after two and a half years of knowing he needed help—finally we could actually get it for him.

We are a family of four of modest means. We work very hard for what we have. I am privileged. I am college-educated. But I cannot afford my son's care without help, and there are so many who need more help than I do. I have type 1 diabetes and my son needs thirty hours of ABA therapy, one hour of speech therapy, and one hour of occupational therapy per week minimum just to give him a leg up in this overwhelming, confusing world. He receives disability Medicaid to help supplement the enormous financial cost of therapy—even with our good insurance, we could never afford his treatment without help. I cried when I was told he was approved for coverage in August. With Medicaid coverage I no longer spend hours on the phone fighting with my insurance over claim denials. With Medicaid my son gets three times as much therapy as my insurance allows—enough help that we are seeing communication and understanding blossom.

My entitlement has changed to humility. I have learned that everything we're given can be taken away. Every time I hear Donald Trump's name I cringe. Is he the undoing of everything that is good?

This month, Emerson started saying, "Hi." He says "Bye" now and "Help me"—and he says, "Mommy," because of the incredible, dedicated, loving teachers and therapists who work with him every day. My son has a lot of goodness to offer this world and we are all working together to get there and already are astounded by his beautiful unique mind and his progress. These wonderful people have changed his life. They've changed mine.

I am having anxiety attacks. My heart pounds. I can't sleep. I already worry about him constantly—his social life, his future, his place in the world. And now I have to worry about him losing the one thing that has helped him more than any other. His therapists, his education. From the moment I knew he existed I knew I would do anything to protect him.

But I don't know how to protect him from this.

My entitlement has changed to humility. I have learned that everything we're given can be taken away.

JOSLYNN, UTAH

Last spring, a boy at my school

called me a c–nt and threatened to rape me as a "joke." This wasn't the first time he'd misbehaved either—he'd groped me before and I'd heard rumors about him doing the same thing to other girls. He was suspended, but a lot of my classmates told me I was being too "sensitive" or that I was a "feminazi" for reporting him. When I saw the video of Donald Trump saying, "Grab 'em by the pussy," I heard John* saying, "I'm going to rape you," and laughing.

The primaries were around the same time, and I was one of the few Hillary supporters at my school—most people liked Bernie—but I was quiet about my position because people would just tell me, again, that I was a "feminazi" who only liked Hillary because we had the same anatomy.

It wasn't until I watched the DNC this summer that I became truly proud to support Hillary. I was particularly moved by the speech by disability rights advocate Anastasia Somoza on the first night. She addressed Trump as exactly who he is: a bully. "I honestly feel bad for anyone with that much hate in their heart," she said.

When Donald Trump speaks, he gives permission for people like John to go from bad to worse. He takes the values of basic kindness and respect toward others and trades them for unadulterated hatred.

When Hillary refused to shake Trump's hand at the second debate, after the *Access Hollywood* tape had just come out, a lot of people tossed it aside as a symptom of the general toxicity of the election. When I saw Hillary do this, I felt her stand up for victims of sexual harassment and assault and declare, "No. This will not be tolerated anymore."

Like many of you, my expectations for Election Day differed from reality. I was heartbroken on November 9 and I am still reeling at the civic behavior of our citizens. But I know from this group, and from my friends and family who are equally appalled as I, that the fight isn't over. The fight is just beginning.

*Name has been changed.

MICHAELA, MASSACHUSETTS

FEAR THIS QUEER!

MEGHAN, NEW JERSEY

I know it's not a pantsuit,

but this is what I wear when I am doing some of my most important work. Being a minister can come with some baggage. Many people in this group have not always had the best interactions with members of the clergy. I carry that burden with me every day. It is a shame that so many ministers have abandoned their role in opening doors and have instead acted like gatekeepers.

I know that this group has members of many different religions as well. I have loved reading your stories, and I thank you for the opportunity to share mine.

I have always tried to be a loving pastor, I have always tried to be welcoming to people of all walks of life. But I never considered the issue of same-sex marriage very much. I wasn't gay, nobody in my family was gay, and same-sex marriage wasn't legal anyway. I know that I was wrong. Unfortunately many people don't realize that yet. This is the reason why so many voters could ignore the fact that a person was misogynistic, racist, homophobic, and xenophobic. Those things don't affect them, so it was far too easy to look past them.

Then one day a woman visited my church and contacted me a few days later to ask me my thoughts on the subject of same-sex marriage. Her granddaughter had met a woman she had fallen in love with and wanted to get married. They wanted to get married in a church and needed a minister to perform the ceremony.

As I was wrestling with my own thoughts on the issue, things were changing in my own life. My wife and I had been struggling for several years with infertility. After many doctors, tens of thousands of dollars, and a lot of tears, we were now overjoyed to finally be holding our beautiful baby boy in our arms. Like all new parents, I spent a lot of time thinking and dreaming about what this tiny little human would someday grow up to be.

So I forced myself to consider what I would do if my son told me he was gay. How would I respond when he told me he had met that special guy he wanted to spend the rest of his life with? Would I welcome this man as my own son? What if they wanted to have children? Would I consider them

continued...

> *It's easy to be judgmental until it affects you or someone you love.*

my grandchildren? Really, these are such ridiculous questions. I was so completely in love with this tiny person that none of these questions really mattered. I wanted the best for him and of course I would want him to enjoy the same benefits all married couples enjoy. I would also want my church to be welcoming to him. If I would want that for my child, I should be willing to offer that to everyone else. Everyone is someone's child. Isn't that what "Love your neighbor as yourself" really means?

That's really the problem with conservative logic. It's easy to be judgmental until it affects you or someone you love.

So I officiated the wedding and it was one of the most beautiful weddings I have ever done.

I am not content any longer to live in a world that doesn't allow everyone access to the same rights and privileges that white, straight, Christian men have enjoyed from the beginning. I think the problem with so many people in my demographic is that they believe that allowing other people to have the rights and privileges they have will somehow diminish what they have. Not only is this false but it is actually harmful. What if the cure for cancer doesn't happen because a smart kid from the inner city couldn't afford college? What if the next breakthrough in engineering doesn't happen because a girl is tired of hearing that her preferred field is a man's field and chooses a different profession?

This society can only be its best when everyone gets a seat at the table. That's why I'm still with her, and I'm with all of you.

AARON, MICHIGAN

Actual conversation

with my seven-year-old son on our way home from school today:

Hudson: "Mommy, Mrs. Evans said a real soldier, a man who went to war, is coming to talk to our class tomorrow."

Me (looking at him through the rearview mirror):

"That man is me, buddy."

It was a genuinely great moment during an otherwise difficult day.

Hillary Clinton: you will always inspire me to be more, to dream bigger, to fight harder. My children are learning that as well. My voice will only get louder.

ADDIE ZINONE, CALIFORNIA

We are people who love and feel more than anyone could know. Even when others don't want you to. Even when others don't approve.

I met my fiancé, Peter, a few years ago, but we recently got engaged.

We proposed to each other and I got him an engagement ring because we figured if we want to be life partners, we should always treat each other the way we would want to be treated. Also, men getting to have all of the fun of proposing is super not fair. He is very tall, blond hair, blue eyes (that I will forever think are gray), and a smile that I can't wait to wake up to for the rest of my life. I, on the other hand, have dark brown skin and very curly natural hair that just gets bigger throughout the day. Race was always an issue for others before the election. He became more aware of the stares we would get, the people blatantly closing the door in my face, the whispers.

And then, Trump happened. And I mean, he really *happened*. We live in a small town in the mountains of North Carolina, where I attend graduate school and Peter works as a student advisor. In other words, we live in a very Trump-heavy, red county. As the election progressed, things got worse. Big trucks with Confederate flags would speed up and slow down behind us as we would walk into the store, the doors in my face became more frequent, the looks more pointed, the whispering louder. I could never be happier or prouder to be with him, but others seem to have a problem with it. People assume we aren't together when we go to restaurants. I was nervous about going to local stores and restaurants right after the election, worried about who would see us and say something. I forget that interracial marriage was only legalized a few years ago. I know other people haven't.

All this to say, Peter is my number-one fan. He encourages me to stay strong, to continue to fight for what we believe in, and to love each other harder every single day. We attend talks on campus about civil discourse. We have friends who love us so, so much, and fight alongside us. We have the most wonderful, supportive families. My mother even went out and bought her first white Santa (which is a huge deal, because she loves her black Santas) because of how important it is to have representation, especially in the family. It's hard, I think, being in a relationship that people don't approve of. Whether it's because you're interracial, same-sex, differently abled, or you identify in a way that people have decided "isn't right," we are still people. We are people who love and feel more than anyone could know. Even when others don't want you to. Even when others don't approve.

This group has become like a family to me. I come here when things feel hopeless, when I'm happy, when I'm pissed. But no matter how hopeless the world feels, we all stand with each other. I couldn't ask for a better community than this.

SHANI-LEIGH, NORTH CAROLINA

This is my youngest daughter,

She is coming up with a plan to help these families.

named after my godsister, 2nd Lieutenant Emily Perez, who was killed in action in September 2006 in Iraq. She is nine and attends a dual-language school. It's a magnet school with many Latino children whose parents are migrant agricultural workers. One of her dear classmates confided that he was afraid he would be sent to Mexico because he and his family "didn't have papers." Emily said she was sad Secretary Clinton didn't win because she would've fought for her friend, his family, and many others like them. She is coming up with a plan to help these families.

This picture represents how she believes that girls can do things to help their friends, family, and country. "We are strong, too, Mommy!" she says.

KIMBERLY, GEORGIA

This is not a
political post.
Just a father and a
daughter. A black
father and his black
daughter. He is
soft. He is tender.
He is loving. He
is not what the
world has told
you he is. Do not
fear him. Embrace
him. Embrace
his daughter.
Overcome. Love.

NJERI, NORTH CAROLINA

Tomorrow

the main program of the American Geophysical Union (AGU) Fall 2016 Meeting begins in San Francisco. This marks my annual pilgrimage up to San Francisco to report my latest results. I am an oceanographer and I work on characterizing the biodiversity of phytoplankton in the ocean using satellite and airborne remote-sensing imagery. As an earth scientist, I am keenly aware of the evidence supporting climate change. Like all earth scientists in my agency, I am very concerned about the incoming administration's willful ignorance regarding this topic and chilling threats to identify earth scientists throughout the government workforce with the implication we will all lose our jobs.

Of course I'm worried about my immediate job future. But that pales compared to how worried I am over the loss of our satellite Earth observations so that we may have an uninterrupted time series of Earth's condition—sea-surface temperature, ocean chlorophyll, atmospheric carbon dioxide, winds, terrestrial (land) vegetation stock and change, land temperature, groundwater stocks, and other parameters relevant to life as we know it on Earth. Continuity in time series data is very important for building and validating models. The US is a leader in Earth observations from space, and we as taxpayers should be proud that

past generations through to the present have supported investment in collecting information about the Earth System. That effort will be squandered in this new administration. If given the chance, the pipeline of trained earth scientists will be drained.

In terms of identity, I fall squarely in the middle of what the inner circle of the new administration vilifies: Latina, highly educated, Seven Sisters alum, pro-choice, nonreligious, Democrat, pro-LGBTQIA, and female. And yet, it is my being an earth scientist and what I know could be lost that has me most concerned at present.

Even so . . . as I prepare my presentation (into the wee hours), I am hopeful. I am hopeful to meet with my fellow earth scientists this week. To learn of their new discoveries in the past year. To hear what they think about the future of earth science in the US. To generate new ideas on how to move forward. To commiserate. I am hopeful that some of us, because it will likely not be all, will still exist as founder populations to reseed the earth science workforce after this administration is over.

Our need to discover burns deeply in each of us, and this coming Dark Age will not extinguish it. I have hope.

I am a white, seventy-year-old veteran gun owner living in Texas.

I drive a red GMC pickup and my favorite music is Texas country and western. I was born in the Little Dixie part of Oklahoma where my family made moonshine and where I learned to cuss so much I make sailors blush. And I am a Roman Catholic. And I have never voted for a Republican and don't see how I ever could.

The best boss I ever had was a woman and I think women should be paid the same as men and sometimes more. I think that what a woman does with her body is no business for old white men like me to decide. I think if two folks love and cherish one another no matter the race or sex then let them get married and leave them alone. I don't hate people because of their religion but I intensely dislike and am suspicious of fundamentalist Christians.

So there. I just wanted the folks in this group to know there are men like me out there even if we are few and far between.

RON, TEXAS

I got to hug Bill!

Just days before the election. This was unforgettable. When he got to me, I thanked him for his support of the disabled community and then this happened. I couldn't stop smiling. I was speechless! Trust me, that's rare!

I'm Mexican, Middle Eastern, gay, and disabled. I use a wheelchair and have spinal muscular atrophy. Doctors said I wouldn't live to be twelve—I'm now twenty-five and the national ambassador for the MDA. My dream is to show the world disabled people are just like anyone else. I want to inspire everyone to live life to the fullest, despite limitations.

I want everyone to feel included in this country. Thanks for listening and creating this wonderfully supportive community, everyone!

JOE AKMAKJIAN, COLORADO

To every person

who rolled down their window and told me to leave this country, to every person who stuck up their middle finger, to every person who belittled me: This is our country too!

Whether you were born in the US like me, or if you're an immigrant to this country, don't let anyone tell you that you do not belong because of how you look or your religious beliefs. There are a lot of good people left in this world who believe in freedom, equality, and justice for all.

Shout-out to all the Bangladeshis!

Shout-out to all the hijabis!

Shout-out to women's empowerment!

(From the newly elected vice chair of the Orange County Democratic Executive Committee, pictured with her friend Sama, the new state committee woman for Osceola.)

NUREN, FLORIDA

I'm from Cleveland, Ohio. I worked for the Obama campaign locally in Cleveland in 2008 during the primary and the general elections of 2008 and 2012. I donated money to Hillary's campaign. I wore this shirt to protest the RNC in Cleveland.

I'm not giving up and neither should you.

MARK, OHIO

Alex was born at 1:24 a.m. twenty-seven years ago today. We lost him way too soon.

Not a day goes by that I don't think about him. Typically, it's my first thought when I awake, sometimes it takes me until breakfast, or my shower, to remember. I fill my life with checklists, but the pain is there each and every day. Alex once told me that we'd be better off without him . . . he was wrong.

This is the picture I have on my phone, one I look at multiple times a day. It's one of my favorites. We got Lexi when Alex was in the hospital back in sixth grade. He helped Alex recover from his eating disorder, and Alex loved that dog fiercely.

I am thankful to those who have been there for us. Thanks for *not* telling us that it's time to move on, thanks for *not* telling us that it's God's will. Our only option is to simply put one foot in front of the other, taking one step at a time, integrating our sorrows into our lives.

I've been privileged to get to know other families over the last few years whose loved ones suffer with opioid addiction, as well as other families who have lost their child to addiction. There is a striking similarity about many of our lost children, their brilliance, their humor, and most of all their sensitivity, almost too sensitive for this world.

I'm fearful for what the future holds for those still struggling with addiction. The recovery system is broken. Please help me to be vigilant against those who promise walls and law and order. We need fewer jails, and more local police supporting diversion programs. We need a greater recognition of the addiction–mental health link. We need more focus on the demand side, and longer recovery programs that actually work.

We need the Affordable Care Act, which provides support for the most vulnerable among us, and we need to ensure insurance parity between medical/surgical vs. mental health services for those of us who do have insurance.

Without these, we risk a rupture in the very social bonds that make us human and keep us civilized.

A wise friend, who also lost a child, told me, "I want my son's death to shape my life, but not define it." I feel that urgency each and every day.

PATRICIA A. ROOS, NEW JERSEY

This is the America I choose.

This is my daughter Karly. Yesterday, she had a tough day; she learned that she had just lost her job. It was a new role as a project lead and she was very excited about it. Due to funding cutbacks, the grant money that had been promised had to be taken back by the state, so, too, Karly's position. She was devastated.

But life goes merrily on its way and so we must do what we do. And off Karly went to get groceries.

A short note about my girl here. From day one, Karly has been the kind of human that has never met a stranger. She is Native American and Anglo. She has deep brown /

black eyes and dark brown hair (well, most of the time—she is twenty-five, it gets colored quite often). But there is something about her that is approachable, attractive, and friendly. People of all kinds talk to her, randomly, often and about all kinds of things, young and old.

Yesterday, as she approached the store, there was a gentleman outside the store, who was cold and hungry who asked her for money to get some food. Karly told him she wouldn't give him money, but she would be happy to buy him something to eat. She didn't say anything to him about the fact that she had carefully planned out her shopping list so that she could get everything she needed with the cash she had just withdrawn from the credit union. Instead, she asked him what he would like to eat.

He said it would be really nice to have a rotisserie chicken since it was already cooked and hot; it was so cold outside. Karly said she would be right back and went in to buy his chicken.

When she came back out, she gave him the food. She also went over to her car and got out a coat and gave it to him.

She then went back into the store to do her shopping.

She carefully went through the store checking off each item on her list and adding everything up so she did not go over the total dollar amount she had in cash. As she proceeded to the checkout lane and was getting ready to cash out, the gentleman behind her in line told her he was going to pay for her groceries.

She was completely caught off guard.

He told her he had seen her act of generosity and kindness to the man in front of the store and he wanted to pay it forward by buying her groceries. He insisted and paid for everything.

This is the America I choose.

Where we craft lives of service toward each other with simple acts of grace and dignity. A meal and a warm coat. An acknowledgment of a kindness.

In the rumble of our differences there are all manner of similarities, all manner of commonalities.

All we have to do is show up and pay attention.

We only lose if we give up.

This is the America I choose, not red or blue but a rainbow of possibility.

EDE, NEW MEXICO

While holding my son,

I finally found the words to voice for the election.

He rests safely in my arms and in this space I can protect him, but with each nap his limbs extend, his voice deepens. He becomes less of my baby, more of my little boy and in the blink of an eye . . . a black man.

Born into a narrative he did not create judged by caricatures of a boogeyman shaped in fear and prejudice and threatening his very existence. I hold him extra tight, whisper I love him, and pray that one day, my boy, my light won't lie cold in the street, alone and scared, blood spilling forth, heartbeat slowing from the 165 that announced his life in my womb to nothing, his killer never brought to justice, his life extinguished like a flame, debated by those that didn't know the power of his smile . . . he *matters*.

Help me! I'm trying to move forward past the looming presidency of a racist narcissist that *you*, my fellow Americans, looked past his hatred and divisiveness and lack of common human decency and said "This is the best America has to offer, this is the path forward, this is *us*," without considering those that look, love, or worship differently than you. As he lines his cabinet with more racist, unqualified, and ignorant leaders, I need you to not only denounce but be active in opposition. This was your vote, it is now your responsibility. The same narrative that threatens my child and American citizens considered "other" by this presidency and validated by your vote has systematically torn societies apart. It takes a village for all our children, I will fight like hell for mine. If you care about our country, our future, you will do the same.

TALAMIEKA, MISSISSIPPI

She was
a beacon
of hope.

Hillary Rodham Clinton became our First Lady

when I was in kindergarten, and she has been my hero my entire life. I was ecstatic when she made New York her home and honored us by representing us in the Senate, and I campaigned for her when she ran for her second term—though I was not yet old enough to vote. I volunteered for her again in her first bid for the presidency, and in my very first presidential primary, I voted for Hillary, my hero. I cried harder than I had in years when she graciously stood up at the Democratic Convention and gave all of her delegates to her opponent, but when she made it clear that she was going to devote *all* of her energy toward ensuring that Barack Hussein Obama would become our country's first black president, I dried my tears and got on board with his campaign.

I, like so many Americans, spent the day of Trump's inauguration completely distraught—it is the cruelest joke that after eight years of unprecedented progress, the clocks would roll back to the 1950s, and what is especially insulting is that 3 million voters were essentially told that their ballots didn't count. I live in the Great State of New York—the Empire State—so I am one of those people. Never in all my life have I been so disillusioned in the promise of America. I skipped the pageantry of the inauguration that day. Out of protest, yes, but also because I just couldn't stomach it.

But I was stopped in my tracks that evening when I scrolled through Facebook and saw an image of Hillary stepping out of her car, dressed in white, a jacket draped over her shoulders like a cape. She was a beacon of hope.

I knew, in that moment, that I had to resurrect my entire Election Day ensemble—from the power suit, to the stars and stripes scarf that I'd used as a belt, to the afro, and, yes, to the baseball tee bearing the most badass *Mean Girls* reference to ever be uttered: "Get in, losers—we're going campaigning." At 6:00 a.m. on January 21, 2017, I pantsuited up in suffragette white, and made my two-hour pilgrimage to Seneca Falls, the birthplace of the women's rights movement, to march.

If Hillary didn't have time to wallow, then neither did I.

LAUREN, NEW YORK

PROTECT:
Black, Asian,
Muslim, Latinx,
Disabled, Trans,
Fat, Poor,
WOMEN

IF YOU
DON'T
FIGHT FOR
ALL WOMEN
YOU FIGHT
FOR
NO WOMEN

On January 21, 2017, one day after the inauguration of Donald Trump, millions of protestors marched in over 900 cities and towns worldwide.

BUENOS AIRES, ARGENTINA

ST. LOUIS, MISSOURI

NAIROBI, KENYA

SEOUL, KOREA

TORRES DEL PAINE, PATAGONIA, CHILE

NOSARA, COSTA RICA

BOSTON, MA

LONDON, ENGLAND

SAN DIEGO, CA

CHICAGO, IL

BARCELONA, SPAIN

LGBTQ+, POC, MUSLIMS ARE WELCOME HERE

CHAPEL HILL, NC

DURBAN, SOUTH AFRICA

NOT THIS PUSSY

UNITY IS STRENGTH

NASHVILLE, TN

ANCHORAGE, AK

MONTPELIER, VT

BELGRADE, SERBIA

OSLO, NORWAY

PRISHTINA, KOSOVO

PARIS, FRANCE

LITTLE ROCK, AK

MESSILA, KUWAIT

BELFAST, IRELAND

OKLAHOMA CITY, OK

BERLIN, GERMANY

SEATTLE, WASHINGTON

SYDNEY, AUSTRALIA

RALEIGH, NC

NEW YORK, NY

Just over three years after I became an American citizen, I marched in Los Angeles: as a woman, a native of Istanbul, Turkey, an immigrant with Muslim roots, a lesbian who came to America to live **openly and freely** in full human dignity.

AYLIN, CALIFORNIA

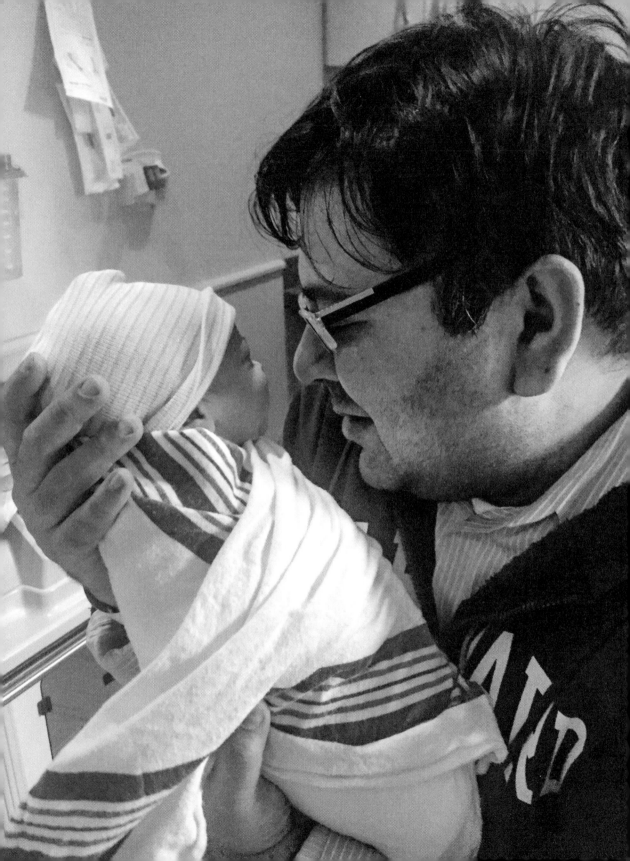

To my newborn daughter,

on the occasion of her birth in a country at a crossroads, my promises to you:

While he builds walls, we'll teach you how to build bridges.

While he abridges our freedom of speech and press, we'll teach you to speak your mind regardless of the consequences.

While he assaults and denigrates women, we'll teach you about self-respect and inner beauty.

While he cuts taxes for the rich, we'll teach you about social responsibility and charity.

While he lines his and his cronies' pockets with taxpayers' money, we'll teach you about things money can't buy, like integrity.

While he rolls back civil rights, we'll teach you that Black Lives Matter.

While he delegitimizes marriage, we'll teach you that love trumps hate.

While he drops bombs, we'll teach you how to plant flowers.

And my last promise to you is that we will never, ever give up.

RAJIB, MARYLAND

A reminder from our daughter that not every chapter has been written...

JAMES & ERIKA, CALIFORNIA

ABOUT THIS BOOK

All written entries included in this book (except one, Aylin, page 252) were originally posted in the secret Facebook group "Pantsuit Nation" between October 25, 2016, and January 21, 2017. Most of the photographs in this book also first appeared in the Facebook group, although some were submitted for inclusion in the book without ever appearing in the group. Contributors, both writers and photographers, submitted their entries for consideration via a secure form outside of Facebook. Each contributor granted full, enthusiastic permission for the use of their words and/or images in the book. All written entries are attributed according to the preference of the contributor and indicated on the page of each entry exactly as they were submitted. Some posts were edited after submission for clarity, consistency, or length, and contributors had the opportunity to review all such changes prior to publication. Sales of this book support the work of Pantsuit Nation and Pantsuit Nation Foundation. For more information, including contributor bios and an archive of stories like those you've just read, please visit www.pantsuitnation.org.

ABOUT PANTSUIT NATION

Libby Chamberlain started Pantsuit Nation as a "secret" Facebook group on October 20, 2016, inviting about thirty of her friends to wear pantsuits to the polls on Election Day. The emphasis on "going high" and a commitment to creating a troll-free space in which Clinton supporters could enthusiastically support their candidate struck a nerve. In the span of twenty-four hours, the group exploded to 24,000 members (new members could only be added by friends already within the group). Within a few weeks, group membership reached three million people.

At the center of Pantsuit Nation is the belief that change—even global, political, tectonic change—comes, first, from the heart. If our country and world are to heal, to bridge our gaps, and to progress forward together toward a more just and inclusive future, we must do something to move the hearts of those who are hardened to the issues facing people who have been historically underrepresented or excluded—people like those whose stories appear on the pages of this book. And, of course, the best way to move a heart is to share a story.

From the outset, members of Pantsuit Nation have shared personal stories, reflecting on why the 2016 election—both as it approached and in the aftermath of its result—was meaningful to them. These stories shine a million-watt spotlight on issues from immigration reform to the rights of people with disabilities, from racial justice to religious freedom, from protecting access to healthcare to the fight for full and unfettered equality for the LGBTQIA community. We are a bullhorn for marginalized voices that can be directed quickly and effectively in response to threats of injustice and oppression.

Pantsuit Nation links the timeless method of using storytelling to drive social and political change with a modern ability to reach a large, digitally savvy audience eager to participate in collective action. We connect our members with calls to action that are focused and easy to navigate, while also providing the context of a story to highlight the immediacy of the need for engagement.

Pantsuit Nation provides resources for educators, human-rights advocates, local grassroots organizations, and the public via our website, newsletter, and other digital content platforms. With the premise that first-person testimonials are our most powerful tools to effect long-term, sustainable change, we are working with impassioned individuals from around the world to build an archive of dynamic, engaging, and far-reaching stories that illustrate, in the most human and immediate terms, how the policies enacted by our governments influence the lives of those around us. Access to these stories gives every member of Pantsuit Nation the tools to become be an informed, emboldened activist.

Collective storytelling has also proven to be an important and needed respite in an emotionally charged and politically fraught landscape, where most online spaces are plagued with combative language, a constant barrage of clickbait, and material that is often hard to fact check or even ascertain an original source. With memes, tweets, petitions, and articles being shared in a flurry of well-intended enthusiasm and urgency, news feeds are often packed with content that is nevertheless void of true human experience. The posts in Pantsuit Nation and the stories shared on our website and in this book are an antidote to the impersonal climate that often dominates political discourse; they provide a window into the experiences of a diverse group of individuals, revealing how policy can affect our everyday lives; and they offer solace and a feeling of solidarity to those who may feel excluded, oppressed, or alone.

Finally, Pantsuit Nation is committed to balancing online engagement with in-person activism. With dozens of local chapters across the country and more forming all the time, we work to connect our members with opportunities to get involved in the political process and in their own communities.

As a reader of this book you are now a member of Pantsuit Nation. That membership comes with benefits—a community of pantsuited warriors to support you, to celebrate with you, to join with you in frustration or in excitement— but also responsibilities. This book must have a life beyond these pages and that life is *you*. Use these stories as a way to engage with people whose views are different from your own. Go out into your community and change something for the better. Run for office. Get involved. Share your own story. Change the world.

Pantsuit Nation is a registered 501(c)(4) nonprofit. Pantsuit Nation Foundation, our associated charitable foundation that supports the work of Pantsuit Nation, is currently under application as a 501(c)(3) nonprofit. For more information, please visit www.pantsuitnation.org.

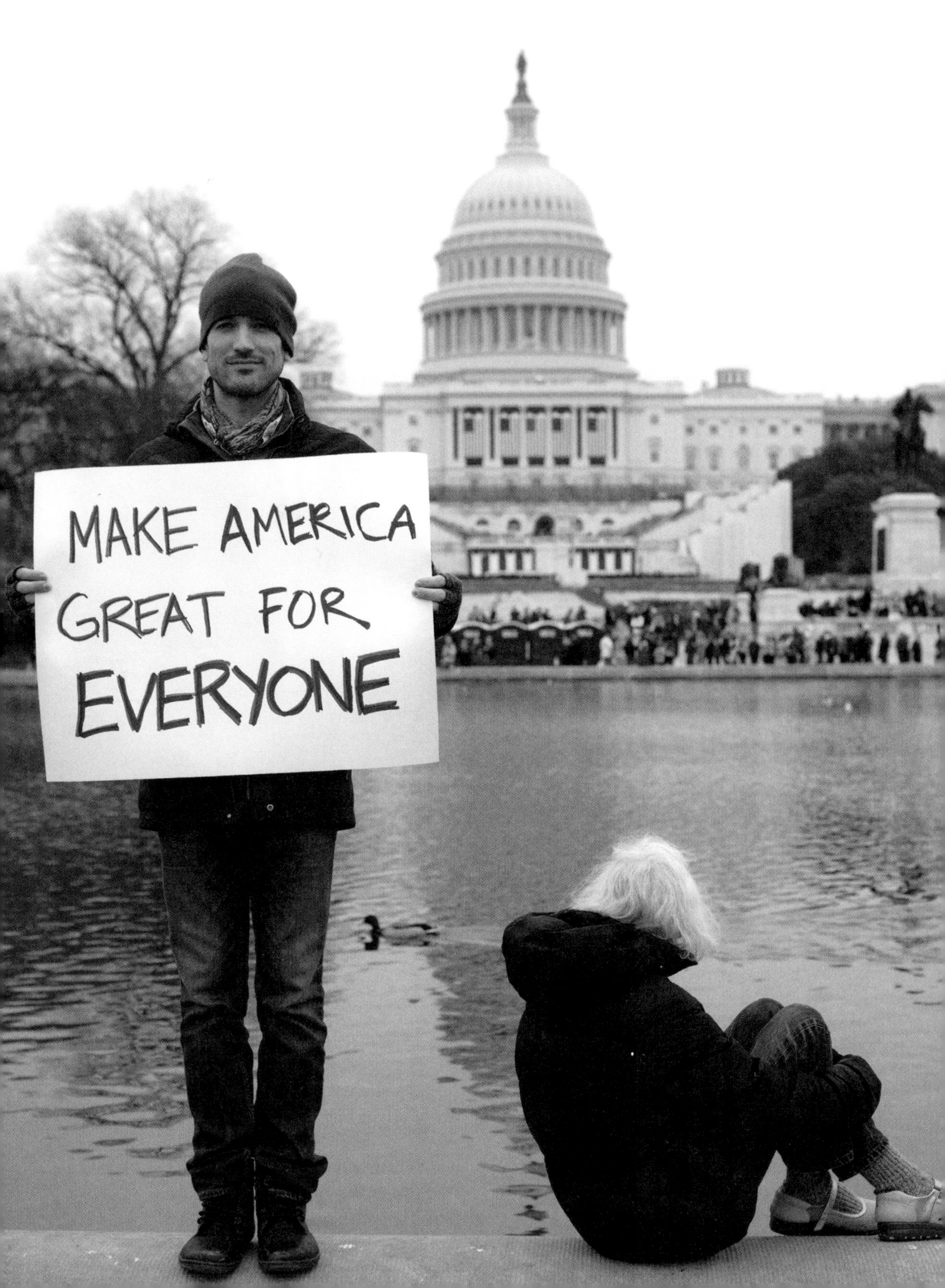
MAKE AMERICA
GREAT FOR
EVERYONE

ACKNOWLEDGMENTS

To Pantsuit Nation members. You are the reason for hope. And to all the contributors to this book. You have entrusted the world with your stories and images, and there is no greater act of courage and faith.

To the Pantsuit Nation moderation team, who have dedicated (and donated) thousands of hours of their lives doing the totally unseen but completely essential work of making the group available and inspiring for millions of people. Each of the stories in this book appeared at one point on a scrolling feed of pending posts in front of one of them and was published to the group with the click of a button. Pantsuit Nation and this book exist because of their efforts.

To the Pantsuit Nation admin team (past and present): Katharine Paolini, Jacky Hayward, Cat Plein, Cortney Tunis, Meghan McCrum, Kimma Barry, Grace Caldara, Antoinette Martinez, Maggie Cook, Amy Kazenegras, Emily Geiger, Libbie Bridge, Kate Wight, Lindsay Watkins, Natasha Muniz, and Kate McCullough, whose humor, commitment, grace, and loyalty have meant the world to me. The pantsuited persisterhood.

To Caddie Jackson, who gave the spark, and who has been an essential and seemingly limitless source of love, support, and enthusiasm since minute one of Pantsuit Nation. And to Lee Fearnside, photo editor, voice of reason, and long-lost summer buddy.

To the partners and families of all those listed above, for bearing with us as we scrolled through our Facebook feeds and group chats at all hours of the day and night. Pantsuit Nation has been operated by women and men sitting by the light of our computers and phone screens while our children slept in our arms or our coworkers glanced sidelong at us or our husbands, wives, and partners kept our worlds (and households) spinning along despite our divided attention.

To Facebook, and all of the engineers and people working behind the scenes to support the explosive growth of Pantsuit Nation, which could not have existed on any other platform in the world.

To Anna Louise Western, Molly Dwyer Blake, and Sarah Morgan Karp, who collaborated on the design of our logo, website, and memes, which in turn inspired the design of this book. And to Emma Mathis, for her research in the earliest phases of this project.

To Jennifer Rudolph Walsh and Margaret Riley King at WME, who shared my vision for Pantsuit Nation from the moment we met and who have been instrumental in helping bring the stories collected here to an audience beyond the confines of a Facebook group.

To my editor, Whitney Frick, for being pantsuited to her core: dedicated, idealistic (in the best possible sense), and courageous. This book might feel solid and real in your hands, but it took Whitney's imagination and commitment to everything that Pantsuit Nation represents to bring it to life. I've gained a friend in the process, and for that I'm also incredibly thankful. And to Jonathan Bennett at Macmillan, whose thoughtful, compassionate, and cohesive design brought together an assortment of Facebook posts and translated them into a collection of voices featured in the most beautiful possible way.

To the entire team at Flatiron Books, who welcomed me completely and with whom I have been so proud to work on behalf of all pantsuited people everywhere.

To friends in Brooklin and beyond who brought us meals, babysat our kids, gave me a virtual high five or a real-life hug, and who encouraged me to keep at it. Especially to Deborah Brewster, Clara Rutenbeck, Ayelet Waldman, and Brittney Carter.

To Patty and V. B. Chamberlain, for their love, generosity, time, and for always saying "yes" when I've asked for help. And to my parents and siblings for a lifetime of support.

To Eleanor and Hugo, lights of my life. The two very best reasons to try to make the world a better place. And to Rick, the invisible engine behind Pantsuit Nation, my most important person, and the one who will always, to me, represent everything good.

Finally, to Hillary Rodham Clinton. Secretary Clinton, this book is for you. Everything you have fought for, all that you have achieved, and all that your candidacy represented to us is truly the heart and soul of Pantsuit Nation. You are one of the original pantsuiters, and always will be. Thank you. We're with you.

"And to the millions of volunteers, community leaders, activists and union organizers who knocked on doors, talked to their neighbors, posted on Facebook—even in secret private Facebook sites—I want everybody coming out from behind that and make sure your voices are heard going forward."

— HRC, NOVEMBER 9, 2016

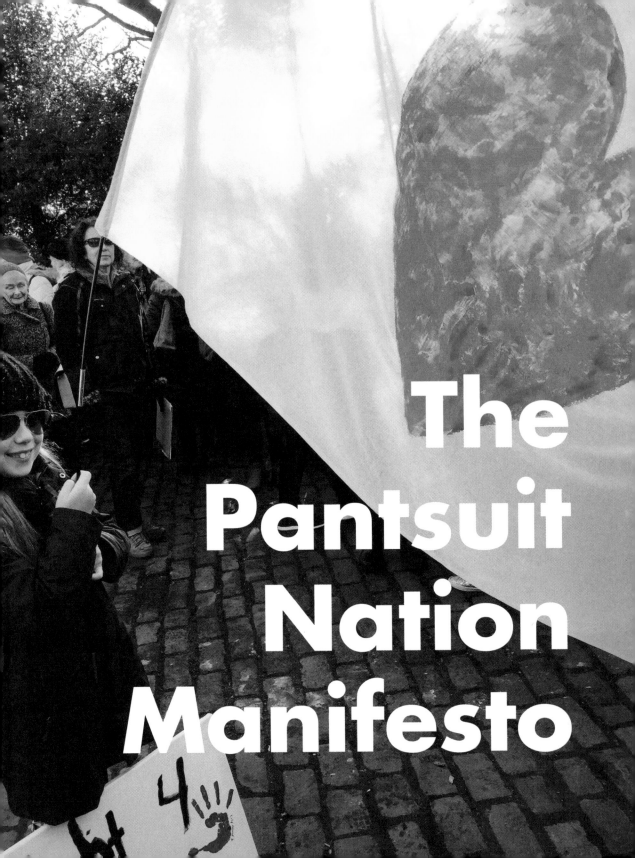

Stories spark change. Taken individually, a story can create a tiny opening in a once-closed space. It is a glimmer. It can shine as something that is true and raw and beautiful. But one story—a single voice telling a single story—is often all too easy to ignore, to shout over or drown out. A single voice can be targeted or silenced.

Pantsuit Nation exists to harness the power of collective storytelling. Millions of voices telling millions of stories. We amplify the voices of those who have historically been underrepresented or excluded. We listen. We empower our members to speak with honesty and without fear of attack. We are strong in our diversity. We invite conversation—*true* conversation—about the issues that are most fundamental to us and our identities.

We believe that feminism is intersectional. We believe that "women's rights are human rights." We believe that progress around racial justice, LGBTQIA rights, rights for people with disabilities, religious freedom, and the fight to combat hatred and bigotry in all forms is most effective when emboldened and humanized through first-person narrative. We believe that politics is personal, and that progressive movement occurs when the empathetic potential of a story is unleashed.

Stories spark change. Taken collectively, stories open us up to the vast and complex realities of what it means to live, work, love, struggle, and celebrate in our country. As Pantsuit Nation, millions of glimmers combine to create the kind of bright light that can't be ignored or overshadowed.

- **Collective storytelling amplifies the voices of those who have been marginalized.**

- **We empower our members to speak with honesty and without fear of attack.**

- **Stories give meaning to action and meaningful action leads to long-term, sustainable change.**

Libby Chamberlain is the founder of
Pantsuit Nation. She lives in coastal Maine
with her husband and two young children.